COTTAGES

AND

MANSIONS

OF THE

JERSEY SHORE

Cottages

AND

Mansions

OF THE

Jersey Shore

CAROLINE SEEBOHM

PHOTOGRAPHS BY PETER C. COOK

RIVERGATE BOOKS

AN IMPRINT OF RUTGERS UNIVERSITY PRESS

NEW BRUNSWICK, NEW JERSEY

Frontispiece: Nestled high on a peak of the Atlantic Highlands mountain range,
the house has a breathtaking view overlooking the boat-sprinkled blue waters
of Sandy Hook Bay. On a clear day you can see New York City.

Page v: Once upon a time, the Jersey Shore was a pristine expanse of marshland and dunes.

Page vi: A Ventnor wharf marches bravely into the rough waves of the Atlantic.

Manufactured in China

Library of Congress Cataloging-in-Publication Data

Seebohm, Caroline.

Cottages and mansions of the Jersey shore / Caroline Seebohm ;
photographs by Peter C. Cook.

p. cm.

Includes bibliographical references and index.

ISBN-13: 978-0-8135-4016-0 (hardcover : alk. paper)

1. Seaside architecture—New Jersey—Atlantic Coast. 2. Architecture,
Domestic—New Jersey—Atlantic Coast. I. Cook, Peter C. II. Title.

NA7575.S44 2007

728'.370974909146—dc22

2006019590

A British Cataloging-in-Publication record
for this book is available from the British Library.

CONTENTS

Simple summer living along the southern shores of Long Beach Island.

ACKNOWLEDGMENTS

This book is the result of the generosity of the many owners who agreed to allow us to photograph their houses and gardens. Without them, there would be no book. Our thanks go to all of them for their hospitality, patience, and support.

The historical societies of New Jersey are an extraordinary resource. Often unsung, they provide invaluable libraries of documents, histories, newspapers, articles, letters, and maps that help create a vivid picture of their region's past. We spent many happy hours in their archives. In particular, we wish to thank Barbara Kolarsick, Rosemary Rizzi, Marie Wingard, and their colleagues at the Spring Lake Historical Society; Carolyn M. Campbell and Linda Kay at the Ocean County Historical Society; and Mary Gruber, Rita Kuhn, Gini Molino, and Suzette Whiting at the Long Beach Island Historical Association.

Robert W. Craig at the New Jersey Historical Preservation Office in Trenton allowed us free access to the voluminous files on historically important houses documented by the state, a rich resource.

Individuals also were extraordinarily helpful in opening doors, making introductions, showing us places we would never otherwise have found, expediting access, providing information (or food) and other generous acts. They include Helen Buttfield, James M. Clark, William and Julie Dunbar, Roy Finamore, Connie Grieff, Renee Guest, Leeann Lavin, Gregory Long, Mary McLaughlin, Daniel Mendelsohn, Annabelle Radcliffe-Trenner and

FACING *Marsh and water welcome autumn leaves at the end of the season.*

LEFT *Stacked boats, like giant insects, point eagerly towards the water.*
BELOW *A classic Jersey Shore battle—a lonely beach holds the line against an army of development threatening in the distance.*

Michael Calafati at Historic Building Architects in Trenton, Yvonne Skaggs, Mary Riley Smith, and Curtice Taylor.

Particular thanks go to Michael and Beth Bliss—Beth especially for sparing a whole day out of her busy life to drive us around Brigantine. We are deeply grateful to Billy Meisch, who tirelessly followed up leads and opened doors in Asbury Park; Tom and Leslie Smith, who lent their boat for photography; Hope Gaines, who found us treasures in Cape May Point; Sandy Henning, whose thorough knowledge of Atlantic Highlands provided us with several excellent locations; and Asbury Park historian James A. Nappi.

Special thanks go to Howard Siskowitz for his contribution to the authors' photograph (with apologies to Edouard Manet's *Argenteuil*), Richard Speedy, Amy Kosh, Taylor Photo of Princeton, New Jersey, and especially to Javier Dauden.

Finally, we should like to thank our colleagues at Rutgers University Press: Alison Hack, Alicia Nadkarni, and, most of all, our editor, Leslie Mitchner, who suggested we do this book.

Lobster fishing is still a local business, dating back to the earliest days of the Jersey Shore.

INTRODUCTION

There's something about the 127-mile-long stretch of coastline stretching from Sandy Hook to Cape May Point that is the essence of New Jersey, in all its beauty, tragedy, toughness, and diversity. Not least of which is its name. A study in 2004 found that the expression "the Jersey Shore" summoned up images of urban blight, hypodermic needles, and gangsters. Yet to those who know it, the Jersey Shore could not be called anything else. The New Jersey Beaches? Ridiculous! The Jersey Coast? Impossible!

The Jersey Shore is unique—a series of close-knit communities that coexist next door to each other, totally divergent in their demographics, interests, architecture, and development, both beloved and hated over the centuries, yet for many the treasured repository of the most blissful memories of summer.

To the fresh eye, unjaundiced by clichés of all-night beach orgies and washed-up medical waste, the Jersey Shore presents an astonishing paradox of untamed marshland and extreme development. It was originally settled, as was much of the state, by Lenni Lenape Indians who fished and farmed its coastal terrain. It was a rough life, with the ocean often threatening the security of the dunes that protected the beach. In 1815, farmer James Baymore lived one mile from the surf in Brigantine. (The site is now out at sea.) It is said that on one occasion during a furious storm, the water came around Baymore's house and would have floated it off its

FACING *Like a Luminist painting, the sky and water of the*
Jersey Shore shimmer in the reflected glory of unspoiled nature.

foundation, but a cow swimming around scrambled onto the porch and its additional weight kept the house stable until the tide subsided.

By the end of the nineteenth century, the Jersey Shore was established as a summer watering-hole by urban Philadelphians and New Yorkers who sought sea breezes and healthy air during the long, hot, humid months of July and August before air-conditioning to some extent alleviated the discomfort. For others, the beauty of the shore itself was enough. White, silky sand stretching for miles along the Atlantic Ocean, with stretches of dense marshland filled with wild animals, birds, and vegetation, created a landscape of almost endless pleasure.

As the railroad inched its way from Sandy Hook down through Long Branch, Asbury Park, Belmar, Spring Lake, Bay Head, Mantoloking, Toms River, Barnegat, Atlantic City, Stone Harbor, Wildwood, all the way south to Cape May, and bridges were built over Barnegat Bay, people began to buy land and build their summer dream-houses. Starting in the late 1800s with a group of prescient Methodists who set up camp meetings in Ocean Grove and South Seaville, the New York rich began gravitating to the geographically convenient northern towns of Rumson, Navesink, and Atlantic Highlands, while Philadelphians and Princetonians made easy trips east to Bay Head and south to Atlantic City. The Irish congregated in Ocean City and Spring Lake, the Jews (often from North Jersey and Brooklyn) chose Deal and Elberon, and everyone else settled wherever they could still find a plot to build on.

Grand hotels were built in these resorts—huge wooden structures with turrets, shutters, gables, and wraparound porches. Equally grand "cottages" arose, favoring in those early years the popular Queen Anne style, which, being both eclectic and complex, lent itself to the extravagant vacation ideal the affluent new residents were beginning to espouse. For the more modest lower-middle and working-class holidaymakers, ranch houses and bungalows sprang up in the shadow of these huge mansions, creating their own communities in places like Brielle and Seaside Heights.

By the end of the twentieth century, much had changed. Many of the vacationing rich were no longer rich, large numbers of the huge summer houses were no longer practical or even inhabitable, and some of the old communities had drifted away or dissolved. Perhaps the most classic case of the altered state of the Jersey Shore was hapless Asbury Park, once a thriving city with a glamorous boardwalk and both summer and year-round homes, enlivened in mid-century by local musician Bruce

Simplicity and grandeur—
reminders of the past glory
of the Jersey Shore.

ABOVE *Old and new face off peacefully in a still-unreclaimed marsh.*
LEFT *The iron claw of development finds a place to dig on every available patch of sand.*

Springsteen, and by the late 1990s a blighted landscape of boarded-up houses, ruined hotels, and crumbling streets.

ABOVE LEFT AND RIGHT
*Pop art at its most colorful
enlivens the streetscape from
Long Branch to Stone Harbor.*

But like the Atlantic Ocean itself, beating endlessly against the white sands, the Jersey Shore constantly reinvents itself. The old cottages and bungalows are being torn down and replaced with fancy new mansions, as in Long Beach Island and the suburbs of Atlantic City; shore real estate is being bought up for parking garages (as in Long Branch); Ocean Grove is more chic, gentrified village than camp meeting these days. Even Asbury Park is slowly coming back to life. While the ocean still devours the beaches on a yearly basis (and residents no longer have cows to anchor their houses), elaborate systems of seawalls, dune planting, and sand redistribution continue to hold the ocean at bay.

Other beach destinations offer nostalgia, but none more powerfully than New Jersey's. The local historical societies are filled with photographs and memoirs describing what has been lost: landmarks razed, houses demolished, beaches terminally eroded. Sometimes it seems that the inexorable drive of development is well on its way to eradicating all traces of the fabulous, frivolous summer places that were once linked like jewels in a necklace from Sandy Hook to Cape May. But memory is a stubborn thing, and what lingers in the minds of those who have spent time here is of communities rich in flavor and personality, side by side, fluctuating over time like the relentless Atlantic tides they embrace. It is the memory of a summer place unlike any other in the world.

The Jersey Shore itself is more than its houses, gardens, communities, or natural beauty. It is, for those who have spent summers there, a rich storehouse of memories that make up an essential part of their lives. "We grew up with its lore of wild parties and easy sex," writes poet Michael Ryan about Ocean City in his autobiography, *Secret Life*; "motel rooms with cold beer in the bathrooms and hot co-eds in the beds, bonfires on the beach and taut, tanned,

ABOVE *A sight summer visitors can only dream about—a December hallucination of vacant parking meters.*
BELOW *A no-entry barrier is powerless against the stunning view of clouds and ocean stretching into infinity.*

bikini-clad beauties undulating to Caribbean rhythms (New Jersey, in my imagination, being transfigured into an island somewhere near Jamaica)."

Or here is novelist Alice Elliott Dark, writing in the *New York Times* about childhoods in Cape May: "Suddenly it was Labor Day weekend, a time of lasts. The last morning at the beach. The last afternoon. The last swim. The last plate of fried tomatoes. The last games with friends. The last night of hearing the sea glass tumbling in the surf. . . . We turned around and waved to the house, the Admiral Hotel, the Coast Guard base, the docks. Then we were gone."

Perhaps it is in winter that the Jersey Shore explains itself most clearly. After Labor Day, as though a bell is rung, the shore closes down. The towns are empty, silent, each one an abandoned paradise, the holidaymakers gone back to their other lives. Faded placards remain—"live bait" on a piece of driftwood, torn menus tacked to a door, an unlit neon sign reading, "vacancy," a handwritten notice, "to rent." Roadside signs still tell pedestrians to face the oncoming traffic, an implausible instruction for these ghostly streets. The old cottages are shuttered, the bungalows locked up, the tents taken down. The strings of traffic lights blink on and off in permanent amber. Even the ocean seems to roll with a muted roar. These shore towns in winter are removed from the world, distant as moons, lapped in shades of gray in the cool silver light, resting, waiting.

For make no mistake. One day in May the lights go on, the shutters are thrown open, front doors are unlocked, children's toys appear in the yard, deck chairs are dusted off, cries and shouts agitate the salty air, pedestrians face the oncoming traffic, and colorful beach towels and bathing suits cling to balconies and railings. The show has started, everyone. It's another summer. Welcome to the Jersey Shore.

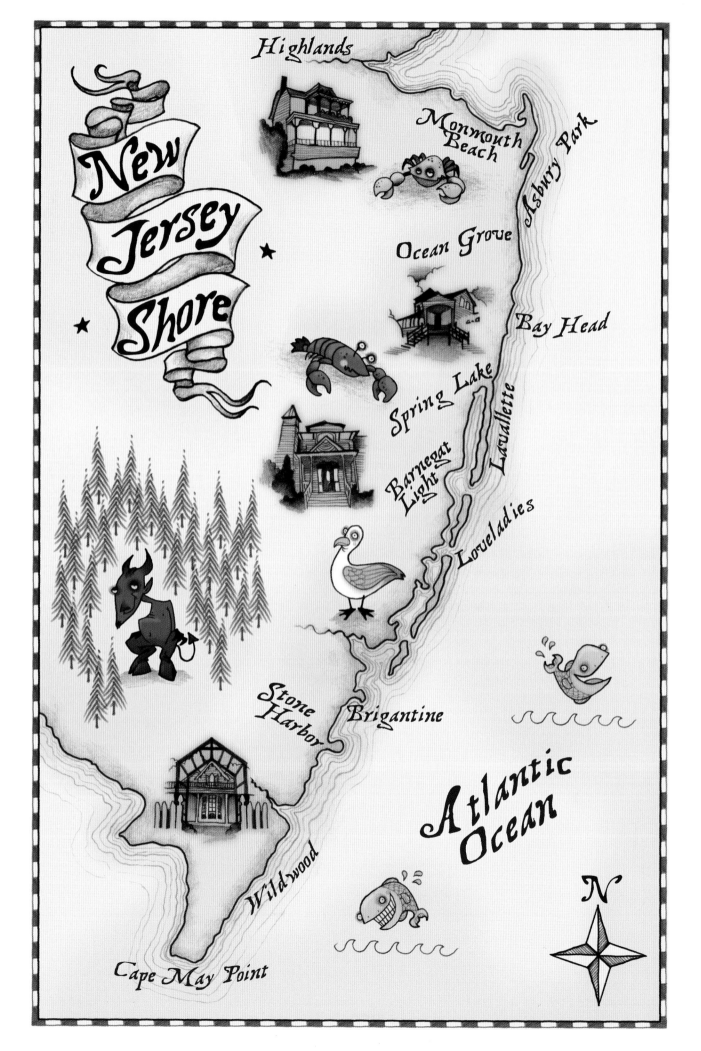

COTTAGES

AND

MANSIONS

OF THE

JERSEY SHORE

Atlantic Highlands

"SOMETIMES I THINK IT LOOKS ENGLISH.
BUT THEN I DECIDE IT'S REALLY PROVENÇAL."

Atlantic Highlands is one of the wonders of the Jersey Shore. As with many areas of this coastline, it was originally settled by Lenni Lenape Indians, who fished and farmed along its creeks and valleys. Fifty-six years after Henry Hudson's 1609 visit, English settlers bought the whole peninsula from the Lenape and called it Portland Poynt. As strife and rebellions altered the political climate, the strategic position of this coastal region soon turned out to be invaluable. The hills in the highlands are roughly 200 to 250 feet high, and although not nearly as high as many mountain ranges in the United States, they are the highest point on the east coast from Maine to Florida, an important topographical statistic that any intelligent general would wish to exploit. This high ground and the dramatic coves and inlets along the shore were witness to many scuffles and engagements between warring settlers, in particular during the Revolutionary War. The retreating British troops passed this way after their 1778 defeat by Washington at the Battle of Monmouth.

As with other nineteenth-century settlements along the northern part of the coast, Methodists scouting the region for summer retreats discovered this lovely spot in the late 1800s, and formed the Atlantic Highlands Association. The religious activities that subsequently took place here throughout the summer months, with camp meetings and other spiritual exercises along with the construction of an outdoor amphitheater and an indoor auditorium, reflect those that occurred in Ocean Grove, its neighbor to the south.

FACING *This Jersey Shore charmer boasts both French and English design features, making it an architectural anomaly amidst its mostly Queen Anne– or Shingle-style contemporaries built in the 1920s.*

Later development was spearheaded by summer vacationers from New York, who, like the Methodists, responded to the extraordinary natural beauty of the area, with mountains and cliffs that tower over views across Sandy Hook and New York Bay. Bringing a more secular atmosphere to Atlantic Highlands, wealthy urbanites built huge estates in the hills and opened up the shore. Sailing became a major entertainment, an amusement park was built, and between 1938 and 1940 the municipal harbor was constructed, which today not only welcomes the yachts of holidaymakers, but has also become a commuter's paradise, providing high-speed ferries to New York eleven times a day.

While many of the great houses of the golden age of Atlantic Highlands were built in the Victorian genre, with Shingle or Queen Anne–style architecture, the occasional anomaly emerges, such as this charming cottage tucked away on a little peak overlooking the enormous blue waters of Sandy Hook Bay. It was built in 1926 for the Brown family of New York, and is now owned by Harriette Dyer Sorensen, known to everyone as Peter, who bought it with her late husband, Sverre, in 1975. Sverre's father was a ship's captain from Norway. Peter and her family summered in Atlantic Highlands, from where her father would commute on the ferry to New York City. Sverre and Peter met on a tennis court in front of the house she now lives in.

Peter admits that the house is difficult to categorize in architectural terms. "Sometimes I think it looks English. But then I decide it's really Provençal." She is right on both counts. Its steeply pitched roof and half-timbered façade are both French and English in origin. What it certainly is not is Shingle or Queen Anne, the style of most of its neighbors constructed at the same period on these mountainsides.

The Sorensens purchased the house after a tragedy. They had lived in a larger house in nearby Monmouth Hills that suffered a fire in 1975 (probably electrical), forcing the family to move. The disaster turned out to have a silver lining, since this house has become as much loved as the one it replaced. Part of the reason is the garden. Both Sverre and Peter Sorensen were always passionate amateur horticulturalists. In Monmouth Hills they not only created a spectacular garden (which was featured in a 1975 issue of *House & Garden*), but encouraged their neighbors to do the same. "When there was a cocktail party—and there were lots in the summertime," Peter recalls, "all the guests would bring a flat of cuttings, and we would exchange them and take them home. This was as well as enjoying the martinis!"

Her husband was also a master woodsman, cutting down trees to let in light and create meandering paths. He built rustic log benches and cut large wood circles for stepping stones. He did much of the digging and especially enjoyed gathering compost from the woods. (Once he and his children gave his wife a truck-load of manure for her birthday. Friends were shocked but she was thrilled!) Sverre loved his woodpile, often making a stack that would block the wind in the winter, thus providing a nice warm place with winter sun (something Norwegians feel very strongly about). The couple liked creating sections that would bloom

Peter Sorensen's garden is full of native trees and shrubs—maples, dogwoods, mountain laurel, azaleas, shadblow—all allowed to grow naturally in a tumble of paths, shrubberies, and dappled light.

together—sometimes moving azaleas in bloom next to rhododendrons under a dogwood, or bunching forget-me-nots and low blue phlox together in a seasonal display.

When the Sorensens moved to the present house, they enthusiastically continued their routine, transplanting azaleas and rhododendrons or whatever they felt should be given more attention, digging compost-rich beds, creating new paths, opening up the woods. Many of the abundant flowers and shrubs were transplanted from the garden in Monmouth Hills. "There were also wonderful native plants and trees already here," Peter explains. "Japanese maples, dogwoods, mountain laurel, deciduous azaleas, viburnums, shadblow, a star magnolia."

Peter inspired her neighbors to get interested in gardening. She also inspired her children, King, Alicia, and Sandy. Sandy (Henning) is now a professional garden designer. After college, she studied landscape design at the New York Botanical Garden, but as she says, "I really learned more from my mother." Accompanied by her beloved dog, Whisper, she mostly works on gardens in Monmouth County and New York City, and still consults with her mother, calling her every morning. "She is a wizard in the early spring," Sandy says, "when everything is appearing. She can detect a weed from the plant—often very difficult. Never does she let anyone weed her garden. And everything is natural—no chemicals touch this garden."

Peter Sorensen is now over ninety years old, and she continues to play bridge regularly and travel widely, having recently completed a trip to Brazil. But gardening remains her first love, and she still saves seeds of foxglove, columbine, lunaria, and other perennials to give away to friends, encouraging them to do what she has done all her life. Such devotion and energy can be felt in the profusion of flower beds and shrubberies that surround the house in a lyrical response to the sparkling vistas of water, city lights, and cruise ships in the distance—a journey for the eye almost impossible to render completely in photographs, as the foliage-framed paths meander up and down the steep slopes, disappearing into shadow, emerging in dappled light round a gully or a clearing.

The house and garden together reflect the rugged landscape within which they nestle. Indeed it amazes the visitor to think how anyone could put up a house in such precarious conditions, particularly a hundred years ago, when even building a road up the steep mountainside was no easy feat. Entering (or leaving) Peter Sorensen's driveway, which is enclosed within narrow stone walls, is not for the faint-hearted. "Everybody hates this driveway," Mrs. Sorensen says cheerfully. "But it's so pretty." Suggestions to enlarge or alter it go unanswered, and her defense is unassailable. Once one has experienced the romance and drama of these lush green hills, who would wish to change them?

"THERE'S A SHORE FEEL TO IT."

Teresa and Joseph DiMattina used to come to the Jersey Shore as children. They would spend summers with his parents, who had a house on Long Beach Island. When Joe's father retired, he bought a house in Atlantic Highlands, and the DiMattinas started visiting there. Teresa and Joe liked the area.

Eighty years ago the Atlantic Highlands coastline was much less developed than it is now. There were a few fishing businesses and shops, and the houses were small and extremely modest. Mostly only local people lived so close to the water, with few summer visitors. Gradually the area was discovered by snowbirds, resort developers, church groups, and town builders. They created the Victorian core of the larger town we know today, attracting thousands of visitors and year-round residents.

The larger and more imposing Victorian mansions were constructed up in the hills well away from the water, because at that time available building materials, in particular glass, could not withstand the violent weather on the shore. Today, of course, materials are much sturdier and houses can be built much closer to the water.

Fifteen years ago, the DiMattinas had the opportunity to buy the house next door to Joe's parents—the waterfront property they had dreamed of. It was a small California ranch-style house, thirty years old, built of brick and clapboard, with three bedrooms. The house had two French doors opening onto a modest cottage deck, and two central fireplaces. The living area was on the second floor, to make the most of the views, with an aboveground basement.

Above all, of course, it had a view—over the Atlantic Highlands Municipal Marina, a landmark. Today this municipal harbor is the largest on the East Coast, home to 715 craft, including a high-speed ferry service to New York City. An iconic view is afforded from the DiMattina house of the ferry trailing a white wake as it ploughs its way towards Sandy Hook, and on over Raritan Bay to the distant shimmering skyscrapers of Manhattan.

Teresa and Joe knew they wanted to expand the house, and refused to buy furniture until the property had been improved. While Teresa was pregnant with triplets, they built the whole house out twenty-two feet, making a great room upstairs with a huge picture window (doors allowed too many stiff sea breezes into the house), and a new kitchen underneath. They put on a new roof, and built a new bulkhead outside to protect against water damage. They added a backyard, with a fence for the babies.

Waterfront property may be the ultimate prize, but shore-owners certainly pay a price for it. In 1992 a nor'easter ripped out the DiMattina's new backyard and roof. Huge waves buffeted the second-floor window. "The water was uncontrollable," remembers Teresa. Her triplets were then three months old. They watched and waited in great trepidation. To everyone's amazement, the great room survived. In fact, the DiMattinas were pleased at how well the house withstood the "perfect storm." Situated in a protected spot, it escaped the worst of the gale. (The marina was ruined.)

Other improvements have since taken place. The DiMattinas installed a swimming pool, and with it another major addition—a garden.

FACING *The path that leads past the side of the house towards the garden is made of crushed oyster shells. The beds are planted with pyracantha and caryopteris, a medley of orange and blue in season.* **ABOVE** *Ribbons of green lawn create a context for the flower beds, and a simple iron railing marks the separation of the garden from the sea.*

"We wanted something to look very special to complement the spectacular views," Teresa said. She turned to local landscape designer and horticulturalist Leeann Lavin, of Duchess Designs, who understood at once the challenge—to make a beach garden that could withstand the salt and ocean breezes that would constantly assault it, and also make it congenial to the extraordinary natural beauty of the site. Leeann is also director of public affairs at the Brooklyn Botanic Garden, so she brings some valuable experience to her garden design work.

Leeann considers garden design as art and always refers to the fine arts for historical context. One of her starting inspirations for this garden was a painting by Monet—*Garden at Sainte-Adresse*. It shows a shore garden with a central open space and beds on each side, with plants offering color along the perimeter. "I was very taken by this design," she says, "how it framed a beautiful view of the sea. I saw how it could be applied here." With Monet's picture in mind, she set about creating a garden that would honor the French artist's charming vision and at the same time work as a practical outdoor space for the DiMattina family.

The close connection between the house and the shore is dramatically evident in the marriage of these two stretches of water. The swimming pool and the Atlantic Ocean seem almost to flow into each other.

The visitor walks from the road down a path made of oyster shells brought in from a South Jersey fisherman's wharf. They crunch invitingly under one's feet, leading towards the waterfront side of the house, and they gleam both in the sun and in the moonlight. "Looking down the walk to the back (ocean) side of the house," Leeann explains, "I designed the side bed with caryopteris and pyracantha. The pyracantha will eventually be espaliered so that the orange berries will look Mediterranean next to the purple blue of the caryopteris. (They will also grow bushy enough to conceal the air conditioning.) Blue lyme grass is at their feet. The blues lead the eye down to the blue of the water."

The garden proper is entered through a gate bordered on either side by tall grasses that stand as beach sentinels. On the right is an evergreen border (left from a former garden), fronted by New Jersey hollies and New Jersey blueberries. "I wanted Teresa's children to learn about some of the great plants that are part of the New Jersey horticultural heritage," Leeann says, "and these are two great examples of the legacy. Plus when the blueberries get shrubbier they will not only fill out the space, but provide lots of fragrance and berries." Leeann's sense of color, like Monet's, is also apparent here: she has selected a variety of reds for the border—dark sweet potato vine, red dahlias, and the red-berried hollies. "The pool beds provide privacy and the framing of the plantings enhances the look of the unbeatable skyline and view beyond the water. The pear-shaped beds contain sun-loving perennials and offer added symmetrical ribbons of plant color when viewed from the upper rooms and decks of the house, with size-scaled plants of Shenandoah red grasses bordered by yellow fern-leaf yarrow, blue penstemon, orange butterfly weed, red geraniums, and pink sea thrift."

Towards the center of the main landscape is an island garden shaped in the form of a teardrop. On one side is the Dinosaur Garden, planted with historically old

plants—gymnosperms, the plant group that includes conifers and related plants such as cycads and gingkoes, along with horsetails. The other side is the Butterfly Garden, with more structurally advanced angiosperms. The two are joined with stepping stones in the form of dinosaur footprints—again to educate and amuse the DiMattina boys. Lawn covers the ocean side of the garden like a smooth green carpet, punctuated by the beds that frame the corner of the yard. A simple iron railing creates the borderline between the garden and the Atlantic ocean, between the elegant man-made landscape and Nature's awesome stretch of open sea.

Although the garden was only started in 2003, it feels already established, a tribute to the designer's skill. There was really nothing there, but now, thanks to Claude Monet and Leeann Lavin, this small coastal garden looks as though it belongs both to the house and to the horizon. "There's a shore feel to it," says Teresa DiMattina. No better compliment could be imagined. 🐚

Trompe l'oeil? No, merely the reflection of the sky in a mirror hung on the wall of the DiMattinas' patio. Magritte would have loved it.

Highlands

" THE WHOLE LANDSCAPE IS NATURE. "

The hill seems impossibly steep. Winding up above Sandy Hook Bay, the narrow road is apparently determined to reach the sky. Wooded enclaves, porches, garden patios, and driveways peek out occasionally from the forested slopes as the climb gets higher. Finally the road opens up and the trees relax their protective canopy, revealing a splendid Colonial Revival Shingle building on the right, and opposite it a house similar in architectural style, with a soaring wraparound porch bookended by two hexagonal pergolas. These twin *tempiettos* and the capacious porch afford views over the forested hillside towards Sandy Hook Bay and the distant shimmer of New York that take one's breath away.

This little mountain, called Monmouth Hill, is one of the treasures of the northern Jersey Shore. It seems not like New Jersey at all, but perhaps California, or the mountains of North Carolina. This vertiginous New Jersey hillside was purchased at the end of the nineteenth century by a group of New York architects who were wise to its exceptional charms, and who joined together to form the Water Witch Club as the core of their planned community here. (The name is from an 1830 novel written by James Fenimore Cooper, entitled *The Water-Witch: or, The Skimmer of the Seas*, a smuggling tale partly set in the rugged waters of Sandy Hook Bay.) The club members, with the prescience that comes from an architectural training, plus a healthy dose of self-interest, thus brilliantly ensured that the place would not be ruined by later development, and that the houses they built for themselves and each other would harmonize with the beauty of the natural environment. The original clubhouse, which was built in 1897 on the left side of the road, soon outgrew its members and was moved to the present site on the right in 1903. The clubhouse was designed by Charles A. Rich, a famous New York architect who, with his partner Hugh Lamb, was responsible

FACING *Perched on the edge of Monmouth Hill, overlooking Sandy Hook Bay, this wonderful old house originally belonged to an architect-member of the exclusive Water Witch Club. One of its most dramatic features is this hexagonal pergola, one of a pair that create bookends for the two-story porch.*

From inside the pergola, a slim wood balustrade is all that lies between the house and a dizzying stretch of forested mountainside leading down to the ocean, and, in the distance, the white skyline of New York.

The view of the house from down the hill accentuates the idiosyncratic architecture with the twin pergolas, like little temples, acting as lookouts for the porches. The ground floor, like all houses built on steep slopes, has several levels, protected by a trellis.

Built from 1905 to 1906, the front façade of the house betrays its Arts and Crafts background, with a columned portico, arched window, and dormer. The architect was F. P. Hill, who built several other cottages on the mountain.

for the Pratt Institute, campus buildings for Dartmouth and Barnard Colleges, and many private residences in New York City. In 1911 the clubhouse burned down, and was later rebuilt in the same style.

The house opposite the Water Witch Club, called "The Hedges," belongs to the Moscatello family. It was begun in 1905 and finished in 1906, to the design of another architect-member of the club, F. P. Hill, who also built several other cottages on the mountain. He adhered to the prevailing style introduced by Charles Rich, that is, Colonial Revival, with Shingle-style variants. Hill's taste leaned towards the Arts and Crafts movement, as is particularly apparent in the interior of the house, with stair railings and inglenook similar to those in another of Hill's houses, the Casino. The portico at the front entrance of the house, with arched windows above it, also reflects the Arts and Crafts influence. But the double-ended porch with its pergolas is the most distinguishing feature of the house. Situated almost at the edge of the cliff, fringed by native plants and shrubs, the porch hovers over the glorious view to the ocean, its balustrades almost giving the effect of the deck of a liner sailing serenely towards the distant port of Manhattan.

The Moscatellos are aware that their house belongs to a long and clubby history. It was almost by accident that they found it in 1989. "My husband wanted to live in a house on a hill," Patricia Moscatello explains. "We decided to drive up the famous Serpentine Road in Highlands, and when we reached the top we saw this house for sale. We bought it within the month."

They made no structural changes to the house, but had to do some renovations for general maintenance. The elaborate woodwork needed repair; and they redid the kitchen and upgraded the plumbing. As for the garden, Mrs. Moscatello admits it is a constant challenge. "There was minimal landscaping when we arrived," she says. "But this is a very difficult place to garden, with the wind and salt air so constantly assaulting the plant material." Deer, she adds, are also a constant presence. The Moscatellos created paths through the woods, planted trees, and extended a patio at the back of the house. "We didn't feel we had to do much," she says. "The whole landscape is nature." Furthermore, as she points out, the garden is at the side and back of the house. Most eyes are fixed on the front, and on the spectacular view that stretches out so dramatically down towards the bay. "The garden must accept second place." People take second place too, humbly and willingly, in this glorious spot. §

Gardening on a mountaintop above an ocean is not an easy prospect. The Moscatellos settled for a series of shady arbors and seating areas surrounded by native trees and plants that can withstand the climate.

Rumson

" MOM KNOWS WHAT SHE LIKES
AND WE KNOW WHAT LOOKS GOOD. *"*

Prominently sited on the Navesink River not far from the ocean is a sprawling wood and brick house of considerable stature and elegance. Built in 1920, it was one of the original Rumson estates built by Bertram Borden, a member of one of Rumson's founding families. Matthew C. D. Borden (1843–1912) came to Rumson in the 1870s with friends and business associates Cornelius N. Bliss and the Reverend Thomas Hastings, and together they bought a large tract of land along the Navesink River that would later be developed into a compound of large summer houses for their families.

Matthew Borden was a textile manufacturer and founder of the American Printing Company, a very profitable organization. He was a big man in many ways; he built an enormous house, "Old Oaks," no longer standing, and he was a friend of the most important families in New York, such as the Phippses and the Guests. He also loved to sail and at one time had a yacht that was the fastest steamer on the Jersey Shore.

His children were equally colorful characters. His son General Howard S. Borden (1877–1950) built more than 150 houses in Rumson, according to historian Randall Gabrielson. Howard was a lot of fun, playing polo, sailing, and hosting singing parties in his barn. Another son, Bertram Borden (1868–1956), was a generous philanthropist, founding with his wife, Mary Owen Borden, a public park in Rumson, Victory Park. He also funded the local high school stadium and scholarships for the students. Both brothers were fascinated by aviation and invested in early flying machines.

The Borden properties stretched from West River Road to the Navesink River. All their estates had fine gardens, with flowers, shrubs, stables, orchid houses, and barns. Many of them have gone, including, sadly, the charming gardener's cottage built for Matthew Borden by Carrère & Hastings (Hastings was the son of Matthew's clerical friend). Originally,

FACING *This magnificent sunken pond, part of the original landscaping, was discovered by the current owners when they began to clear the land of its long-neglected jungle of undergrowth.*

Bertram's long, low-lying clapboard house was on six acres at the eastern end of the family land, with many bedrooms and bathrooms and a large garden tended by thirteen gardeners. Bertram was a major local benefactor, and his house, called "Riverlands," was the center of several civic events, including the annual Rumson Garden Show Awards.

At some point between its completion in 1873 and 1917, the house burned down. It was completely rebuilt, half in wood and half in brick. It is thought that the house was originally all wood, and the Bordens sensibly decided to rebuild at least part of it in brick so that it would be less vulnerable to fire, while retaining the look of the original clapboard. The re-built house was finished in 1917, judging by the date stamped on a copper downspout that presumably was one of the last features of the house to be completed.

The patio, roughly fifteen thousand square feet in size and elegantly laid with brick masonry, was built by the Hellings family to replace a lawn and knot garden. The long cedar pergola is original.

*A semicircular bench,
garlanded with hydrangeas
in late summer, is
original to the property.*

The Hellings family bought the house, with six acres, in 1977. Both Brian and Ann Hellings came to New Jersey from England, which perhaps explains their energetic transformation of the very neglected garden. While keeping many of the original features, including a four-hundred-year-old tulip tree (there was a second that they lost), a Hinoki cypress, two crape myrtles, plus linden and beech trees, they extended the property and made some additions, including trees (four Scotch laburnums, magnolia, and two redwoods, among others), an organic vegetable garden, an orchard, a greenhouse, lawns, gravel paths, borders, fruit bushes, and flower beds.

"When we got here, it was in very poor shape," say James and Charles Hellings, two sons who help look after the property. They remember as children peeking through a brick wall

ABOVE *Much beloved of the two Hellings*
sons, the vegetable garden they created
is very prolific—and all organic.
RIGHT *A stone wall attempts to contain*
the profusion of annuals and perennials
planted by the front door of the house.

This view from the rooftop overlooks the back garden, showing its size and sweep.

and feeling quite scared at the jungle that confronted them. As they cleared the land over the years, they found many charming original landscaping elements, such as paths, flower beds, stone benches, wrought-iron railings, a magnificent sunken pond, and perhaps the oldest swimming pool in Rumson. They also kept other architectural features, including pergolas, garden gates, and the original gardener's cottage with its copper roofing and cast-iron lamps.

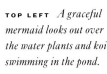

TOP LEFT *A graceful mermaid looks out over the water plants and koi swimming in the pond.*

TOP RIGHT *On the northwest side of the house, facing the river, is a glamorous shell-like fountain, original to the house. Its bowl, glowing almost like amber in the light, is made of a single piece of limestone.*

BOTTOM LEFT *The pool, which lies within splashing distance of the Navesink River, is perhaps the oldest swimming pool in Rumson.*

BOTTOM RIGHT *The roof is made of original Welsh slate. The tall Elizabethan-style chimneys and fine copper gutters are also original.*

There was originally another residence on the property, which Mr. and Mrs. Hellings partly razed, turning the rest into garden storage and creating more acreage. They also built a completely new brick patio on the northwest side of the house, facing the Navesink River. (It was originally a lawn and a knot garden.) The patio is very large, perhaps fifteen thousand square feet, and provides a wonderful venue for entertaining and enjoying the sunset. The fountain, its bowl made of a single piece of limestone, is original to the house, as is the long cedar pergola, which seems never to have had to sustain any climbing plants (such as wisteria or grapevines), hence its remarkably good condition. (A similar pergola at the far end of the swimming pool has been damaged over time by climbing vines.)

Although the garden is spectacular in its design and variety, the house is up to the challenge, its mixture of Georgian and Elizabethan architecture perfectly at home in this dramatic landscape. The roof is made of Welsh slate (immensely difficult to repair), the handsome chimneys are original, and the fine copper gutters recall its early origins.

"There's no master plan here," James Hellings explains, looking back at the house from the pond where koi fish swim around in the sunshine. "Mom knows what she likes and we know what looks good. It's an ongoing process."

Monmouth Beach

"I LIKE IT WHEN PEOPLE SAY IT LOOKS
AS THOUGH IT HAS ALWAYS BEEN HERE."

Making a garden on the beach may seem an oxymoron. It is famously difficult to grow plants in a place where salt air, fierce winds, and extremes of temperature are the norm. But microclimates have a way of abolishing these obstacles, and in a small lot two blocks away from the shore on Cook Street in Monmouth Beach, a lovely small garden has grown up despite itself, offering a combination of trees, shrubs, flowers, and vegetables that would be expected to flourish in only the most protected corners of the world. The owner of this little garden miracle is Mary Rogowski, who, as a regional director of a scientific software company, works a great deal of the time at home, and therefore is able to enjoy on a daily basis the views that are presented to her when she looks out of her windows.

The magician behind Mary's little landscape is Leeann Lavin, who produced the DiMattinas' garden overlooking Sandy Hook Bay, a windswept lot that she carefully planted both to enhance the yard in front of the house and also to encompass the majestic view. For Mary's garden, the challenge was different. Being to some extent protected from the shore, the garden could handle a more complex range of plantings. But lacking the dazzling natural beauty that the DiMattinas' site offered, Leeann had to find a way to create a visual experience that would work as well, but in a different way, for her client on Cook Street.

As all good landscape designers know, the garden should tell a story. It should also relate to the house, and in this case, the house was a sweet inspiration. It is only three and a half

FACING *One of the seven* potagers, *or vegetable gardens, each one with a different theme and separated by peat gravel, combining flowers, vegetables, and herbs, and anchored with roses and boxwood.*

years old. Prior to its construction, the previous home, a one-story ranch, had been removed along with its Victorian garden. Living across the street, Mary had the advantage of watching the new house evolve to the design of local architect James Monteforte. As the Low-Country style typical of South Carolina, with its cedar shakes and wraparound porch, took shape, she knew she wanted it. Although the house was rather larger than she had in mind (it has three bedrooms), "I took the plunge," she says, and bought it from the builder for herself.

"It has a wonderful quality," she explains. "I saw the wraparound porch of the Low-Country style as an extension of the inside space and knew it would be perfect for dining and entertaining." It also has the feel of an old-fashioned Victorian bungalow—the perfect starting point for a garden.

"I had grown up on a street with lovely gardens," Mary remembers. "We always enjoyed working with plants. Our town house had planters with flowers and vegetables everywhere. Gardening runs in the family. My great-grandmother was an herbalist and grew all sorts of healing plants in her garden. My grandparents also had a wonderful garden, with lots of fruit trees. I can remember collecting and preserving cherries that were served as a special treat over ice cream during the holidays. I used to follow my grandmother around, planting bulbs, picking lily of the valley and daffodils."

These were surely distant memories as she surveyed the derelict lot that opened up on the south and west sides of her Victorian cottage. There was nothing that could possibly remind her of her childhood gardens, except perhaps the presence of some Atlas cedars and other mature trees in lonely splendor. Otherwise, it was just a flat expanse of scrappy grass. Mary was not downcast. "Here was an opportunity," she remembers thinking. At first, she started slowly. She contacted a landscaper and asked him to make her some beds and to plant a few big trees and shrubs as infrastructure. "But I wanted something more creative," she says. "Leeann had the visionary mind I was looking for."

Mary was not short of ideas herself. She loves cottage gardens in England, and liked the idea of mixing vegetables and flowers that she had seen there. She also wanted an area near the kitchen for herbs and vegetables that would not be sectioned off as in so many gardens. Another requirement was that she should be able to bring flowers into the house throughout the season—"affordable luxury," as she calls it. Leeann Lavin, with her own knowledge of English gardens (she has been on more than a dozen tours to the great ones), and her skill in understanding a difficult climate, responded to Mary's requests with a brilliant series of solutions.

"From a design standpoint, the front yard was long, but quite narrow—less than twelve feet wide. Sitting with Mary in her welcoming kitchen/living room area, and noting the wraparound porch, I couldn't help but think part of her dream garden would be to include a *potager* or kitchen garden—and that concept was fueled by learning that Mary loved to

The low-lying house with its wraparound porch, typical of South Carolina architecture, is a perfect foil for the tiny but extensive garden that has been given life by garden designer Leeann Lavin. Here a Moorish-style rill extends outwards from the side porch, framed by green lawn and bordered by bluestone.

entertain. Looking out of her kitchen window, I realized we could design a beautiful garden that was also practical—varied but simple."

As Leeann points out, many Americans are not aware that a combined herb and vegetable garden has a long horticultural history and can make a beautiful ornamental contribution to the landscape. "I divided Mary's *potager* into seven three-foot plots, distinguished by color or theme, each in a formal rectangular or circular shape, separated by pea gravel. These plots are anchored with box and roses on the street side (Mary loves the combination of box and roses), next to the existing white picket fence. I chose *tuteurs* for structure and planted red hyacinth beans, which I call my 'magic beans,' to provide a key vertical design element when viewed from the street and kitchen and living room."

The first plot is anchored by a smoke bush. Its red hue amplifies the red-themed plantings of dianthus, rhubarb, chives, and asparagus. The second bed is lavender, surrounding pink phlox and pink baby's breath in the center. "Mary added strawberries here and they look delightful." Winnie, her Westie, finds them a tasty afternoon snack. The center plot is the widest, with two kinds of mint—chocolate and pineapple—planted on an axis, surrounded by fragrant pink alyssum. Next a patch of tricolor sage, purple sage, and rosemary, followed by the "pizza garden"—New Jersey tomatoes, oregano, and basil. "Then we come to yellows—New Jersey corn and golden oregano, followed by the melon garden, with melons, pumpkins, and watermelons, positioned on a vertical "ladder" to garner more growing area in a limited space, and finally a helianthus border to add fall color."

The fieldstone walkway is interplanted with lime, thyme, and coccineus, so that as you walk you release the perfume of the herbs. The side yard (on the east side of the garden) is called the Hydrangea Allée, with Sky Pencil holly, hydrangeas, low box, and ivy. "I like it when people say it looks as though it has always been here," says Leeann.

The side yard is the largest part of the garden, and has been given drama by the addition of a rill, reminiscent of a Moorish canal, bordered by bluestone, with aquatic plants and fish. Mary also wanted some white noise to offset neighboring pastimes and suggested the three bubbler fountains that can be turned on and off at will. There are three border gardens: The Butterfly Color Garden features perennials such as acanthus, aconite, echinacea, liatris, and candytuft. The back of the garden—the White Garden—is elevated by soil dug out to make the rill, with exist-

Clustering around the picket fence, Mary Rogowski's flowers and shrubs, including the vertical red hyacinth beans, give a welcoming wave to passersby.

ing trees plus ferns, azaleas, winter-blooming camellias, heuchera, lady's mantle, and hundreds of white spring-blooming bulbs. The Rock and Grass Garden is planted with various grasses, yucca, sedum, winter heaths, and heather. "These were chosen to take the afternoon heat in the summertime and add structure and balance."

To think that this elaborate landscape was created in under three years is quite remarkable. The rill, the walkways, and the garden beds were accomplished with the skill of Burke Honnold Landscaping, whose teamwork, says Leeann, "encompasses years of experience and respect for the unique and distinctive look of the area's native garden design."

The garden is enhanced every year by annuals, carefully chosen for color and scent. Thus throughout the year the garden offers an abundance not only of flowers but also of fruit and vegetables—the "affordable luxury" and year-round interest that Mary had hoped for. Providing such beauty and variety in a small space, plus the very real issue of "protection" from extremely close neighbors, while countering the prevailing climate of salt air, wind, and heat, created a challenge that Mary Rogowski and Leeann Lavin responded to with triumphant results.

Allenhurst

*"*I DIDN'T WANT TO LET ANYONE TOUCH THE HOUSE
WHO DIDN'T KNOW HOW TO RESTORE IT PROPERLY.*"*

Monmouth County is the county on the New Jersey Shore closest to New York, and much of its coastline is occupied by the homes of wealthy New Yorkers who discovered it in the nineteenth and early twentieth centuries. The Gilded Age mansions that decorated the towns between Asbury Park and Long Branch were built by distinguished architects of the period, such as Stanford White, who enhanced the properties with their signature touches of French, Italian, or English design that so pleased the rich clients they served. Some of these great cottages have since been torn down, but they have been replaced by equally spectacular ones, for the new millionaires of the late twentieth century quickly learned what their forerunners had discovered. The pleasing nature of these exclusive shore resorts and their ease of access from New York City made them as desirable to the new generation as they were to the old.

Deal, Elberon, Allenhurst—this group of contiguous communities along the eastern shore of Monmouth County is like a baroque music trio, sedate in manner but graceful, elegant, and determinedly stylish. The overall look of these towns is subdued, with no fast-food or souvenir shops offending the wide and serene sweep of the tree-lined boulevards. The houses are often built on small promontories high above the street, or concealed behind tall hedges and walls. A few families with children stroll along the sidewalks during the summer season, but most of them prefer to entertain themselves in private within the large estates that have been created for them, enjoying the generous shady porches and landscaped gardens of which few casual passersby catch even a glimpse.

A corner property in the center of Allenhurst is a fine example of the standard of architecture demanded by taste and money a hundred years ago. Sited one block from the beach, it was built in 1911 by Aarons Builders, a family of local architects who had many commissions for private houses between Asbury Park and Long Branch. Mr. Aarons and his family

FACING *The entrance is suitably imposing with its original wrought-iron gate, brick pillars decorated with stone quoins, and globe-shaped finials. It opens onto a magnificent staircase leading up to the front door of the mansion.*

ABOVE *A view of the porch, which wraps around the south and east sides of the house, with Chinese Chippendale balustrades.* **RIGHT** *Different materials affect the house like abstract art.* **FACING** *The south-facing porch, paved in black-and-white marble, evokes the splendor of the Italian Renaissance. Blue-and-white striped canvas curtains add summer lightness and a sense of intimacy.*

The pool, completely redesigned by the owner, is protected by a high hedge and decorated with Italian statuary and containers of flowers.

lived in it themselves for twenty-five years before selling it. The house was owned by two other families before Alex Adjmy bought it in 1992.

The house is grand—grand in vision, grand in stature, grand in execution. The architect favored the Italian Renaissance style, and every aspect of the structure reflects this theme. The long, three-story building has wide overhanging eaves with decorative roundels, bracketed roofs, dormer windows with Moorish arches, square and round columns, bay windows, wrought-iron balustrades, and a vast porch that runs along the front and east side of the house, paved in black-and-white marble. The entrance gate is wrought-iron, supported by brick pillars with stone quoins and topped with carved balls. The wide stone steps leading up to the front door are flanked by statues. French doors on the north side of the house open onto the pool; the pool pavilion has a bay window, a colonnaded porch, and a second-floor balustrade; the garden surrounding the pool is planted with flowers and shrubs and protected by a high brick wall. The stucco façade of the house is white, and it gleams in its Italianate context like a Florentine jewel.

To achieve this effect was not easy. When Mr. Adjmy bought the house it was in a sad state of disrepair. Almost every column, floor, bracket, and eave had to be restored or replaced. Every square and round column had to be stripped to its original mahogany and then painted in its original color. All the wrought-iron railings decorating the exterior of the house had to be re-fashioned. Old carriage doors were reinstalled. The entire roof was changed from

ABOVE LEFT *A canopied bay window, with original balustrades, looks out over the pool.*

ABOVE RIGHT *The view from the east end of the pool shows the curtained exterior of the pool house and patio, with Chinese Chippendale woodwork decorating the second-floor balcony.*

ABOVE *The main façade of the house shows its debt to Mediterranean architecture—pillars, wide overhanging eaves, decorative roundels, and, on the third floor, dormers with Moorish arches.*

LEFT *A cornucopia of architectural styles: round and square columns and wide bracketed eaves create a fascinating contrast with the detailed artistry of dentils and roundels.*

asphalt to slate. The pool was redesigned, and the modernized pool house restored to its former glory. The copper flashing was recast. The list seems unending, and in fact it has been continuing for ten years.

Moreover, Mr. Adjmy, who is in the apparel business, is no easy client. Everything had to be done perfectly. "One of the most difficult things was finding the right craftsmen," he explains. "I didn't want to let anyone touch the house who didn't know how to restore it properly."

The interior was an equally daunting challenge. "All the interior paneling was painted over," Mr. Adjmy says. "We had to strip it down to its original mahogany." Floors and doors were also stripped. The kitchen was entirely redone. Bathrooms were replaced and restored to their original look, using copies of the original hardware. "Original" is a favorite word in Mr. Adjmy's lexicon. "I enjoy everything old," he admits. "Old cars, old houses, old furniture." He attends auctions to find the objects he requires, including the handsome Italian statuary in the garden.

Although he owns two other homes, for most of the summer he lives in the Allenhurst house with his three sons, as well as on weekends and holidays throughout the year. "I have almost got it to the point where I am comfortable here," he says. He loves the house with a passion, and one suspects he will never be completely satisfied. Some houses are like that. "I have been to at least seventy or eighty beautiful homes in my life," Alex Adjmy declares. "But nothing compares to this."

The owner's appreciation of stone and marble garden ornaments is evident in this composition installed against the north wall of the pool garden.

Asbury Park

THE STORY OF A SHORE TOWN

Asbury Park is not for the faint-hearted. Its history is as chequered as a NASCAR flag, and just as gritty. How many statements from local politicians over the years have been uttered about its "renewal"? How many reams of newsprint have been focused on its "revival"? What exactly is the problem with Asbury Park?

It started like a fairy tale. In the mid-1800s, when the Jersey Shore was being discovered as the next-best thing to paradise for summer vacationers from the big cities to the north and west, William B. Osborn bought up a piece of wooded beachfront in Ocean Grove as a summer home for his Methodist flock. James A. Bradley, a New York entrepreneur (and practicing Methodist), heard about Osborn's purchase and, inspired, bought a piece of Ocean Grove for himself. Visiting the property later, he decided he did not like it (see pp. 55–56). But being a shrewd businessman, he saw its potential, and instead, in 1871, he bought up five hundred acres of the shore immediately to the north for ninety thousand dollars. This time the investment paid off. He developed the land and created a small city called Asbury Park, in honor of Bishop Francis Asbury (1745–1816), the founder of the American Methodist Church.

The place was an immediate success. Situated between three lovely stretches of water (Wesley Lake, Deal Lake, and Sunset Lake), with a mile-long boardwalk, a well-planned downtown with wide leafy boulevards, and at least eleven fine churches, Asbury Park was a number-one vacation spot for New York and northern New Jersey through the first decade of the twentieth century. In 1916 its assessed valuations were nearly double any other municipality in Monmouth County. During the years after its founding, it grew from a small village to a major town, with a Convention Hall and Theatre (including a Hall of Nations), a Casino and plaza, a solarium, a new and wider boardwalk, a country club, the Palace

FACING *This poignant image of a deluxe hotel's fall from grace tells the story of Asbury Park's tragic history.*

43

Fragments of fun palaces provide clues to the revival of the boardwalk.

Amusements, a sprightly local newspaper, storm jetties, hotels, apartment buildings, and Steinbach's, which opened in 1912, "the largest resort department store in the world." Cotton candy was Asbury Park's most famous product. Even a devastating fire in 1917 could not slow down the town's energy and enthusiasm.

Best of all, the town council came up with the greatest children's event of them all, the Asbury Park Baby Parade. The first parade took place on July 22, 1890, and by the 1920s it was so famous that the governor of New Jersey and celebrities from stage and film—even presidents—attended this annual summer extravaganza.

So what happened? How did this thriving community morph into a sad, run-down shell of itself? How could this beautifully situated shore town, with its lakes, lovely houses, grand public buildings, and elegant boardwalk, so lose its reputation? How could a resort that measured itself favorably against any of its neighbors, from Deal to Spring Lake, decline so dramatically? Where did Asbury Park go wrong?

Many wise observers offer reasons. "Dropping property values, and a growing dominance of one-stop shopping centers led to the town's character changing," suggests author Ben Ruset, in an article for NJPineBarrens.com. The building of the Garden State Parkway diverted holidaymakers from Asbury Park to other resorts. The new residents of Asbury Park, attracted by its easy amusements and lively entertainments, came from less educated or moneyed classes, changing the social profile of the town.

The seeds of its decline may have come earlier, even at its birth. As far back as 1889, historian and musicologist Gustav Kobbe, in a book about the Jersey coast, described the anxieties of neighboring Ocean Grove when the Asbury Park land first came up for sale. The Methodists feared that it might fall into the wrong hands, Kobbe explained. Bradley was a hero, since not only was he a devout churchman, but "he gave no deeds without a clause against liquor-selling." This was a noble gesture, but Kobbe, an astute observer, saw ripples of disruption lurking beneath the optimistic façade of the newer community. "So far resembling Ocean Grove," he commented, "Asbury Park in other respects conforms to the world, and stimulated by the fiery influence of ice-cream and ginger-pop, its permanent and floating population may plunge into the vortex of social dissipation afforded by pool, billiards, bowling, smoking and dancing."

Billiards! Bowling! Smoking and dancing! The devil was at the doorstep. Three years later, Stephen Crane also sensed a strange misalliance between the two towns, describing in an article in the *New York Tribune* in July 1892 the "great train-loads of pleasure-seekers and religious worshippers" arriving at the huge double railway station of Ocean Grove and Asbury Park. As the years passed, the juxtaposition of God and Mammon along this tight strip of the Jersey Shore turned into something more problematic, as Ocean Grove retained its austere rules well into the 1970s, and Asbury Park turned more and more to what Kobbe foresaw, a destination of pleasure run wild.

In the 1950s and 1960s Asbury Park still held powerful attractions. People remember going there, enjoying the cotton candy, the amusement palace, the boardwalk arcades, the carousel near the Casino, and the huge crowds who flocked to attend the rock concerts at the Convention Hall. For bored teenagers on vacation with their parents, Asbury Park offered the kind of garish entertainment that promised "fun for all."

The iconic roofline of Howard Johnson's is one-of-a-kind.

Rock-and-roll had a regular home in Asbury Park, and its most famous performer, Bruce Springsteen, sang through the 1970s in the Stone Pony, formerly Palace Amusements, above the picture of Tillie, the grinning clown, that had been a landmark of the town since 1956.

But by that time the town had fallen apart. Thanks in part to a thriving Ku Klux Klan membership established since the 1950s, in the summer of 1970 race riots in Asbury Park lasted for five days, and forty-six people were shot. This started a downward spiral that was perpetuated by a long and painful saga of bankruptcies, corruption of and by city officials, fatal business decisions concerning the future of the town, a string of dishonest developers, and even the mayor, Dennis Buckley, caught buying cocaine in a sleazy bar opposite City Hall. In 1989, after yet another failed redevelopment project, the municipality itself declared bankruptcy.

Since 1990, reams of newsprint have insisted that Asbury Park is on the way back up: "Boardwalk Is Symbol of City's Renewal"; "Asbury Park's Long Recovery"; "At Last, Asbury Park Starts to Awaken"; "This Development Plan, Officials Say, Will Return Asbury Park to Glory Days." Hope springs eternal in Asbury Park, it seems.

One of the biggest new purchasers of beachfront land, Asbury Partners, promises condominiums, town houses, and retail space. Another developer, Metro Homes, is rebuilding Ocean Avenue. Other entrepreneurs are taking long, hard looks at the town. The idea is to turn 450,000 square feet of oceanfront land into a vibrant retail center that will attract visitors once more, transforming Asbury Park into its original mixture of grand buildings and democratic entertainments.

Meanwhile, visitors today to the beachfront of Asbury Park are unlikely to believe what

ABOVE *A former beauty parlor built in the 1930s was converted into an elegant private home for businessman Robb Levinsky.*

TOP RIGHT *This fascinating pink house is both modern and traditional, with specially made wrought-iron railings decorating the second-floor balcony.*

RIGHT *Bright blue paint gives this classic summer cottage the look of a festive holiday house.*

BELOW RIGHT *A fine example of circa 1910 Arts and Crafts architecture, this year-round house is owned by Asbury Park's foremost historian and supporter, Jim Nappi.*

BELOW *With a quote by Thoreau stenciled on the façade, this Art-Nouveau bungalow, built in 1921, has an Asian-inspired garden created by local politician Kate Mellina and her husband, David Christopher.*

they see. It looks like a scene from a post-nuclear disaster—a few boarded-up shops and eateries, peeling signs with lost letters promising incomprehensible delights, stuffed garbage bins acting like magnets to screaming seagulls, and, at each end of the boardwalk, two once-glorious buildings, the Convention Hall and the Casino, stare each other down like raddled divas, trying to conceal their shattered façades. As author Daniel Wolff says in his new book, *4th of July, Asbury Park: A History of the Promised Land*, "it wasn't really a city at all, it was an amusement." An amusement that had gone terribly wrong.

Asbury Park hopes for more than shoe repair.

There is something almost heroic about the fact that in the twenty-first century, when every handful of sand on the Jersey Shore is as valuable as a pan of gold, and where every developer worth his dollar signs is zeroing in on the last few lots still available for building up or tearing down, Asbury Park should so defiantly have continued to fend off the devouring hordes.

Some residents agree, and believe that the future is finally going to be as golden as the beach they cherish. A number of gays and lesbians have moved into Asbury Park, and their influence is already noticeable, in the form of house restoration and redecoration, and the opening of several new restaurants and bars. Furniture dealer Billy Meisch (called "the King of Asbury Park" by Bruce Springsteen) believes that Asbury Park has finally turned the corner. After living in Ocean Grove for several years, Billy moved to Asbury Park in 1980 and took several doses of disappointment as corruption and financial disasters continued to prevent the town from moving out of its economic quagmire. But now, having opened an elegant modern and vintage furniture store on Cookman Avenue (the street where the venerable Steinbach's once stood), he is sure that the time is right.

When he bought his house in 1980, there was only one other establishment on Cookman Avenue, apart from abandoned buildings—a pawnbroker. Now Cookman Avenue is part of the central plan for Asbury Park's future. Way back from the haunted boardwalk, along wide, tree-lined avenues to the north and west of the town, pretty nineteenth- and early-twentieth-century cottages are being bought up and restored.

"It's different now," Billy declares. "People are buying homes, not just investing in commercial property. Real estate prices are taking a leap upwards, a sign that people are prepared to commit to the place, to live here. And some of the houses in Asbury Park are very attractive, having withstood the overbuilding fad that has spoiled many other shore towns."

THE ANGEL HOUSE

One of the most well-known supporters of Asbury Park is Thomas O'Leary. Like many Asbury Park residents, he is committed to this shore community. Currently executive director of the Samaritan Homeless Interim Program in Somerville, Tom has had a colorful past, including being the lead singer for a band called Steel Tips that performed at the legendary Manhattan club CBGB. His partner, Danial Anderson, found 401 Seventh Avenue in 1977 and purchased it for himself and his mother. "Right after the riots," Tom O'Leary points out. When Danny's mother died in 1991, Tom moved in.

The house at 401 Seventh Avenue was one of those originally owned by the town's founder, James A. Bradley, and dates from 1884. It was added on to in the 1890s, and survived a series of owners and economic ups and downs, including being transferred in the Great

LEFT Cherubs hold up a platform in charming imitation of the caryatids of the Acropolis in Athens.
RIGHT "I always thought a garden should be a collection of pictures," explains Tom O'Leary. He has achieved his goal, producing a verdant gallery of art.
FACING Gilded angels flying high indicate to the passerby that this is indeed "the Angel House."

ABOVE *The house, dating from 1884 and originally owned by the town's founder, James Bradley, has taken on a brilliant new life since the 1990s. With its peach, coral, and yellow façade, it seems almost to be blushing at the exuberant garden that surrounds it.* **RIGHT** *A lion guards the entry to the garden.*

Depression for a dollar. Since the 1990s, however, it has been lovingly restored by its two owners in a way that James Bradley might have found somewhat startling.

The colors of the house are very provocative. "I love color," Tom confesses. "We have used Georgia peach, Key West coral, and Navajo yellow." But it is the garden, originally a barren patch of earth, that stops traffic. Danial planted trees such as maples and evergreens for privacy. Tom was after a more dramatic effect. "I always thought a garden should be a collection of pictures," he explains. "So our garden has four different entrances with four different views and vistas, each with a focal point that draws the eye into the garden." The planting is eccentric but effective. "I hate square and oval bushes—they're so sterile," Tom declares. But Danny likes topiary, so Tom has found a way to make parts of the garden look like a Tudor parterre.

Over the last decade, as the painted angels and pillars and statuary started appearing, people began to talk. "Everyone thought we were crazy," Tom says, "but now they are all doing it." Tom's passion is for medieval art and history, and he loves classical architecture. "I like to pick up statues and sculptures in antique stores and markets in the winter, when prices are down. Of course they are all damaged in some way, otherwise I couldn't afford them!" But when Tom comes home with yet another disfigured lion or goddess, his friend Danny, who worked at the Metropolitan Museum of Art in New York, is quick to say, "Well, how often do you see a complete Greco/Roman statue in a museum?"

Disliking the square, formal look, the owners installed a circular gate like a moon gate, planted blowsy beds and containers, and tucked in the obligatory statuary to fill in gaps.

The garden is also a memorial to lost Asbury Park. Tom scavenges for materials abandoned by the town. The circular marble pieces, for instance, come from the demolished Albion Hotel, and the bricks around the pond were rescued from a roadwork project along Seventh Avenue. Each year more treasures are discovered and absorbed into this idiosyncratic landscape. "People ask, 'You're still adding?'" Tom says. "I call it progress."

This Asbury Park garden is a metaphor for the town itself, transforming from a black-and-white canvas to a riot of color and life. Teenagers walking past the house once said it reminded them of Dorothy's house in *The Wizard of Oz*, which dropped from the sky. Other people call the house "The Angel House" or "The Embassy." Tom and Danny call it home.

◈◈◈

"I LOVE ITS SUMMER COTTAGE ASPECT."

Are we in New England? Nantucket perhaps? The old-world charm of this house, with its portico, shutters, dormers, pretty English garden, and serene lake in the background, can surely not be within hailing distance of the Jersey Shore.

The surprise is that not only is the house on the Jersey Shore, but it is also in that most unlikely of towns, Asbury Park.

Asbury Park, among its many other qualities, dubious and otherwise, has the unique distinction of being situated between three lakes. This topographical anomaly creates the extraordinary effect of having wandered into a village in the English Lake District. The streets are small and quiet, without fast-food stands or souvenir shops, and the houses looking over these peaceful stretches of water are as serene as the water itself. One cannot quite hear the roar of the Atlantic Ocean a few blocks away, and the air seems remarkably fresh and clear in these pockets of lakeside living.

The house was built in 1929, and, like most of its neighbors, was designed as a year-round house for people who lived and worked either nearby or in the cities of New York or Philadelphia. The owner, a banker, was not planning to buy in Asbury Park (who would, with its reputation?), but when he saw the house in 2003 he fell in love with it. When he bought it the house was covered in vinyl siding; there was no portico or picket fence, and no porch or gazebo in back. In its favor, in the owner's opinion, was its fine position at the end of a street, and a gorgeous view of the lake.

With the help of the New York–based architectural firm of Wagner Van Dam, the house soon assumed the look of a proper summer cottage. The architects built a wide back porch and gazebo along the rear façade, respecting the wood trim of the original screen porch, so that the elegant old carpentry work was given prominent play in the new configuration. The owner now had a proper place to be outside and enjoy the view. A garden was planted with shrubs, a water fountain and small pond, and beds with spring and summer flowers. The house was recovered in clapboard and painted gray, and a picket fence was added, the perfect surroundings for a dream house by the sea. "I love its summer cottage aspect," the owner declares.

The result is a delightful rural retreat that indeed could have sprung from Nantucket, but better yet proudly belongs to that much-maligned, struggling eyesore of a shore town, Asbury Park. Who would ever have guessed it?

ABOVE *A charming gazebo, added by the owner when he bought the house in 2003, makes the most of the lovely view across one of Asbury Park's three lakes.*
RIGHT *The rear of the house was transformed by opening up the porch and adding the gazebo. The fretwork on both sides of the staircase, original to the 1929 screen porch, was carefully preserved.*

Ocean Grove

"THE SINGING ALONE IS ENOUGH TO
SWEEP DOWN THE POWERS OF HELL."

Even people who think that the Jersey Shore is another way of saying Overcrowded Tourist Dump must acknowledge that Ocean Grove is special—a magical town built by a group of people who may have devotedly spent time with God in church throughout the year, but who also knew where God would probably most enjoy spending a couple of months in the summer.

This little community was founded in 1869 as a Methodist camp site by minister William B. Osborn, who had been looking up and down the shore for some time to find a summer retreat for his flock. Troubled farther south by hordes of mosquitoes, he had the good fortune to find this piece of unspoiled beachfront land, surrounded by forests of native New Jersey trees (pine, cedar, and hickory)—with the inestimable advantage of "the absence of disease-bearing mosquitoes."

Thus the Ocean Grove Camp Meeting Association of the Methodist Episcopal Church was born. Its first president was Ellwood H. Stokes, who remained in office from 1870 until his death in 1897. A statue in the main square memorializes his tenure. The Association's stated mission was "to provide opportunities for spiritual birth, growth and renewal through worship, educational, cultural and recreational programs for persons of all ages in a proper, convenient and desirable Christian seaside setting." The Methodists thus inspired came to Ocean Grove in droves every summer, put up their tents, and attended to their religious duties by the side of the spiritually neutral but beautiful Atlantic Ocean.

This "desirable Christian seaside setting" was transformed, then, into a tent village. Although today that has sad connotations of refugee camps, in those days tents were the only form of shelter for visitors to this totally undeveloped part of the state. The whole shore, in fact, was one huge empty campground. James A. Bradley, a New York businessman and a

FACING *The classic forms of the cottages of Ocean Grove are an architectural delight.*

55

In the summertime, the canvas "tents" are ablaze with color.

devout Methodist, heard about Osborn's purchase and bought a piece of land in Ocean Grove for himself, sight unseen, for eighty-five dollars. In 1870 he visited it for the first time with his black servant, John Baker. They pitched their tent and slept under the stars with their heads resting on cushions retrieved from their horse-drawn carriage. They were quite alone. "Not a soul was within hearing distance of us," Bradley reported later. His servant did not like the emptiness. "Mr. B.," he sighed, "this is a wilderness place." (Perhaps Mr. Bradley felt the same way. In 1871 he bought five hundred acres of land less than a mile away. It became Asbury Park.)

Ocean Grove did not long remain a wilderness. In 1887 it was described by the *Asbury Park Press* as "nomadic dwellings cozily ensconced under the foliage." Its coziness, wonderful white beaches, and cheerful surf were a big draw for the Methodist faithful. But for all their efforts towards spiritual birth, growth, and renewal, the temptations of a summer on the Jersey Shore clearly became an issue. In order to maintain "proper" behavior from the flock, strict laws were passed by the Association. No liquor, of course. No dancing. No card-playing. No theater. No carriages on the beach. No parades. No unseemly dress. On Sundays the rules were even stricter, in compliance with the holiness of the day—meditation and prayer only, no vehicular traffic, no bathing on the beach, no shops open, no newspaper delivery, no hanging laundry outside. On Sundays, the gates of Ocean Grove were closed to all but locals going to church (which one was required to attend twice).

In spite of (or perhaps because of) these severe strictures, the popularity of the summer prayer-resort spread, and in 1894, the Great Auditorium, a massive ornate wooden structure with turrets and other Victorian ornamentation was built, big enough to accommodate seven thousand of the faithful. President Ulysses S. Grant attended its dedication. By this time the tents had been replaced by more permanent structures, neat rows of modest one-story cottages made of wood, with one or two rooms front and back. Small porches were protected by canvas awnings like a tent (thus retaining the key element of the town's

The winter appearance of these wooden cottages provides an austere, almost abstract beauty.

origins), where families could sit and enjoy the sunshine—with the Good Book on their laps, of course.

The Camp Meeting Association retained control of all the real estate in Ocean Grove. It leased out the cottages to Protestants only, with a letter from one's minister required to prove it. Nobody could buy property; and each tent was passed down through the family. Other Victorian-style cottages were built, with room for larger families, but the traditions remained. The blue laws were sacrosanct. Church-going, revivalist meetings, and serious meditation were the order of the day. Many famous visitors, including Presidents McKinley, Roosevelt, and Taft, and summer residents spilling over from Asbury Park, came to look at the Methodists and their odd ways. Stephen Crane, who spent a lot of time at the shore, wrote that the Methodists "greet each other with quiet enthusiasm and immediately set about holding meetings."

Yet there's something about summer at the shore that makes even the most devout congregation a little skittish. A description of frolicking Methodists comes down to us from a charter member of the Camp Meeting Association: "The surf lubricates the joints like oil; grave men fling out their limbs like colts in pastures; dignified women, from the very inspiration of necessity, sport like girls at recess." Another eyewitness vividly describes his impression of the summer residents letting off steam during their hymn-singing: "If you want to hear such singing as you can hear nowhere else this side of heaven, go to a live Camp Meeting at Ocean Grove," a preacher reported. "The singing alone is enough to sweep down the powers of hell."

These intimations of exuberance were perhaps a sign of the times. As surely as tides ebb and flow, this strangely controlled and controlling society came under threat as Americans flexed their secular muscles in the second half of the twentieth century. In 1972, a newspaper delivery company sued to start delivery in Ocean Grove on Sundays. This was the beginning of an entirely new era for Ocean Grove. Suddenly lawyers, realtors, and developers began to scrutinize the extraordinary domination of the Ocean Grove Camp Meeting Association over its little paradise—its blue laws, its restrictions on entertainment, its dress code, its private police force, its real estate monopoly. In 1979, after many legal battles, the New Jersey Supreme Court held that it was inappropriate for a religious organization to have such overwhelming power, and Ocean Grove lost its charter, becoming part of Neptune Township.

Many people in Ocean Grove were outraged. "It was a small community of religious people," says Scott Thompson, a longtime resident. "This ruling changed everything. Till 1979, we did not need zoning. When that ruling brought down the old regime, the old families started selling out and gradually the place filled up with new people with no religious affiliation."

Other old-timers feel the same, and many are still supporting efforts to secede from Neptune Township and return to the good old days, but in fact their worst fears have proved unfounded. The "new people" may not have been religious, but most are respectful of the history and the architecture of the town.

One of these is Van Wifvat, who came to Ocean Grove in 1995 and bought a two-story

The house was covered in phony brick when Van Wifvat bought it. He removed it to reveal the original clapboard and painted it a delicate, creamy pink.

Victorian Stick-style house with elegant fretwork detailing. It was one of the earliest houses in town, dating from roughly 1872. "It was a romantic cottage designed in the Asian style that was fashionable then," Van Wifvat explains. "Much simpler than the more ornate Victorian-style houses that were built later." However, it had been seriously "improved" by its previous owners, with a façade of asphalt brick, much interior overpainting, and garish vinyl panels stuck up everywhere to conceal faulty plastering and moldings. All the French doors and double-hung windows were nailed shut and covered with mini-blinds.

"Not being a Methodist," Wifvat observes, "I didn't know anybody in Ocean Grove. I had always been in the Hamptons or the Catskills. The town was unfamiliar to me and the house was a wreck. But I fell in love with it."

Van Wifvat is an owner of the New York design firm Van Gregory & Norton, a fortunate profession for someone embarking on the complete reconstruction of a wreck. He stripped the phony brick from the exterior, revealing the original clapboard façade, and painted it a delicate, creamy pink. Inside, he took off the bright red and orange vinyl tiles, patched the walls, opened up the doors and windows, remodeled the kitchen, and exposed the door frames and moldings and opened them up. The living room shows off what was once a coal-burning stove, an unusual installation. Most of the other houses on his block, inhabited only in the summertime, did not have fireplaces. Now painted subtle creams and beiges, with a dark forest-green trim for the door frames, the cottage seems to gleam serenely in its late-Victorian renaissance.

The demographics of Ocean Grove are different now. Many city-dwellers (particularly

This is one of the oldest houses in town, dating from roughly 1872. It is a less complex version of the Victorian Stick-style houses built a decade or so later, although the fretwork balustrades and elegant roof trim have the delicacy of that architecture at its best.

ABOVE *Van Wifvat worked hard on the interior to bring back its simple charm, such as opening up the doors and windows, stripping woodwork of layers of paint and walls of tile, and repairing damaged moldings.*

RIGHT *The kitchen was remodeled almost entirely, with the addition of plain pine furniture and a collection of white dinnerware, thus reviving the old cottage atmosphere that had converted the owner to Ocean Grove in the first place.*

New Yorkers and Philadelphians), with or without religious affiliations, are moving into this unspoiled and quiet town for a summer retreat, just as the Methodists did almost 150 years ago. Many of the houses have been restored and repainted (although longtime residents complain of the plastic and vinyl materials used as siding, and the continued habit of enclosing porches). Antique shops and restaurants have sprouted up everywhere. In the Great Auditorium, where Methodists once sang their heads off in praise of the Almighty, now the Preservation Hall Jazz Band and Garrison Keillor perform to the cheers and applause of agnostics and atheists.

Traces of the Camp Meeting Association's legacy remain. Ocean Grove is still a "dry" town; no liquor can be bought here. The land must still be leased from the Association. The street names retain their religious history: Mount Tabor, Mount Hermon, Bethany, Mount Zion, Mount Carmel, Pilgrim Path. Bible classes and Christian youth programs are much in evidence. If you own a tent, no more than seven people are allowed to stay overnight, and no pets, open fires, or barbecues are allowed. Originally there were 600 of these extraordinary miniature mansions; now only 114 remain, but even with these restrictions, there is a fifteen-year waiting list for a lease. (Outside one tent is stitched the sign, "Home Sweet Tent.")

But the most dramatic change to the town reflects the massive social shift taking place throughout the United States. The first "new people" in Ocean Grove were gays and lesbians, who found this quiet summer resort a refreshing change from the craziness of Fire Island or the Hamptons. Now homosexuals live in elegantly restored Victorian cottages next door to old-time Methodists, who by training should be praying daily for the souls of their neighbors. It seems, however, that not only can revivalists and revisionists live side by side in this lovely town, but that the irony is understood and appreciated by all.

Spring Lake

Of all the communities along the Jersey Shore, Spring Lake is considered one of the most beautiful. The number of late nineteenth-century mansions (known as "cottages") lining in stately glory the avenues from Ocean Road to South Boulevard dazzle the eye. If Cape May is paradise for the gingerbread and "painted lady" set, Spring Lake compares in elegance and exuberance to the great building booms of Newport and Bar Harbor. Like those famous resort towns, Spring Lake became the second home to a set of rich summer residents from Philadelphia and New York, including presidents and inventors, financiers and politicians.

The area, like so many beach towns, was originally a small community of fishermen and farmers living around the natural spring lake called Fresh Creek Pond. But the success of the Methodist venture at neighboring Ocean Grove inspired developers to explore a little farther south, and a group of them came together to build a huge hotel called Monmouth House in Spring Lake Beach. The hotel, completed in 1876, was one of the biggest yet built along the shore. It had 250 rooms, a dining room that seated one thousand, and a steam elevator. It was built, as T. E. Rose wrote in 1878 in the *Historical and Biographical Atlas of the New Jersey Coast*, "in the most substantial manner, broad piazzas, large well ventilated rooms, electric calls in every apartment, in fact possessing every convenience that can in any manner add to the comfort of its guests." President Ulysses S. Grant was one of the more famous early guests to enjoy these comforts. (In 1889, the room rate was $3.50 to $4.00 a night—the going rate for a first-class hotel.)

Meanwhile, an adjacent piece of land, called Brighton, was expanded by Joseph Tuttle and William Reid with the addition of another hotel, called Wilburton-by-the-Sea. It is now called The Breakers, on Newark and Ocean Avenues. A tract farther to the north, called

FACING *The dizzying proportions of the front entrance, with its steep flight of stairs, semicircular double-storied portico, twin columns at each level, and decorative eaves, announce to the world that this is a house to be reckoned with.*

63

One of the most spectacular examples of Spring Lake architecture, the Maloney Cottage has an exuberance that marks it as the personal statement of one of the most important founders of the town. He was Irish business entrepreneur Martin Maloney, who purchased the house in 1898 (and then promptly built a bigger one close by).

Como, surrounding what is now called Lake Como, adjacent to Belmar, also became a target of development.

While many of the large hotels burned down, suffering the fate of so many wooden buildings along the shore in those early years of expansion, Spring Lake, incorporated as a borough in 1892, continued to attract summer residents. Not only did the town offer convenient transportation to and from the cities to the west and north, but also the original lots were generous in size, thus allowing a lot of room for architects to exercise their imagination and for landscape designers to fulfill their dreams of palatial garden art. The fantastic range of architectural styles expressed in Spring Lake during those explosive fin-de-siècle years still has the power to astonish the contemporary visitor.

Many of the early settlers were Irish, and Spring Lake is often called, appropriately, the Irish Riviera. An Irish accent is still a familiar sound in the town, and as for the appellation "Riviera," the gorgeous late-nineteenth-century mansions that still stand in the face of modern development are a reminder of Spring Lake's early movie-star glamour as a summer resort. Indeed, Spring Lake still inspires the creative imagination; Hollywood came to Spring Lake in 1980, when parts of the movie *Ragtime* were shot here, and mystery writer Mary

The shore-facing façade shows the architecture of the house in all its profligacy— columns, Palladian detailing, balustrades, canopies, brick pedestals and chimneys, and irregular rooflines.

Higgins Clark has had a second home here since 1998. As she told Bill Finlay, a *New York Times* reporter, "I just love to sit on my porch, relax, and look at the ocean."

One of the most spectacular examples of Spring Lake architecture is the so-called Maloney Cottage, at 101 Morris Avenue. Its wedding-cake opulence, fantastical porches and verandahs up steep flights of stairs, elaborate carpentry, curved balustrades, and dizzying rooflines cause people today to stop and stare. Brilliantly white, intricately decorated, the house represents the Gilded Age of Spring Lake at its most glamorous.

It was built around 1890 by an unknown builder, and was purchased in 1898 by Martin Maloney (1848–1928), one of the early settlers of Spring Lake and a prominent member of the expanding summer community. At the same time Maloney built another mansion nearby with the Irish name Ballingarry, which he moved into in 1901. An Irish émigré, Maloney left school in Scranton, Pennsylvania, at the age of twelve to work in the coal mines. In his twenties, he became involved in the technology of gas street lighting, and with the arrival of electricity, he alertly transformed his business into the Philadelphia Electric Company. The enterprising Irishman did not stop there, acquiring interests in oil companies, railroads, and real estate ventures in Pennsylvania and New Jersey.

Maloney liked Spring Lake, and invested heavily in real estate in the town. His biggest building venture was his own mansion, Ballingarry, which was designed by the distinguished Philadelphia architect Horace Trumbauer, a favorite of the socially prominent Main Line family, the Stotesburys. Ballingarry was much bigger than 101 Morris Avenue, and after Maloney and his family had moved into the bigger house, he rented out the cottage to summer visitors.

In the same year, 1901, Maloney contributed another major landmark to the town—St. Catharine's Roman Catholic Church, named for his daughter, Catharine, who died of consumption (now called tuberculosis) in 1900 at the age of seventeen. Again he enlisted Trumbauer to design the building in what is described as Italian Renaissance Revival or Romanesque style. It was patterned after St. Peter's Basilica in Rome, where, according to Barbara Kolarsick, president of the Spring Lake Historical Society, the Maloneys had sent their sick child, vainly believing, like many American and English families during this period when consumption was an epidemic, that she might find a cure there for her illness. (The heroine of Edith Wharton's short story "Roman Fever" makes one of these sad pilgrimages.)

In 1908, Maloney deeded 101 Morris Avenue to another daughter, Margaret. It was rented by Joseph P. Tumulty, private secretary to President Woodrow Wilson from 1913 to 1921, and the president spent several summer weekends there. Ballingarry, the big mansion, was torn down in the 1950s, but 101 Morris Avenue survived. It passed down through several owners, and since 1985 has been in the loving hands of Mr. and Mrs. Lawrence Larkin. Martin Maloney died in 1928, having left his mark (and enhanced the reputation of the Irish) in spectacular fashion upon the town of Spring Lake.

HISTORY RESIDES AT THE KATZENBACH COTTAGE

In a town filled with architectural flights of fancy, none represents the romantic style as well as 200 Madison Avenue, a house tucked away behind dense shrubbery a little way from the shore. Its history is like a short and brilliant survey of American politics, and in particular of one of the most important families of New Jersey.

Known as the Katzenbach Cottage, it was built in 1890 as the summer home of Frank S. Katzenbach Sr. (1844–1921), whose father, Peter, came to the United States with his family in 1824 from Katzenbach, Bavaria. Peter Katzenbach was a friend of Napoleon's brother, Joseph Bonaparte (1768–1844), formerly king of Naples and Spain, who had emigrated to

Nestled behind dense shrubbery, the Katzenbach Cottage combines romance with architectural ingenuity. It was built in 1890 as the summer home of the Katzenbach family, a name that resonates in American history. The architect was H. E. Finch, who chose the wonderfully eccentric Queen Anne style for his important client's vacation house.

A conical "pepperpot" turret on the east side of the house, with dentil points under the brim, is flanked by dormers and gables.
An elegantly carved pediment at the front door reflects the extensive ornamentation that decorates every façade of the cottage.

ABOVE *With the variations of roofline, chimneys, and ornamented gables, combined with the dazzling shingle patterns, the house presents a textbook of architectural styles.* **RIGHT** *Spindle columns and balustrades create a delicate boundary for the most unusual variety of exterior shingles, most of which would be impossible to replace today.* **BELOW** *The curved porch, with its graceful balustrades and spindles, adds a feeling of old-world charm to the cottage.*

The Rizzis are only the second owners of the cottage. They made very few renovations, besides planting a lovely flower and vegetable garden behind the house.

North America and built a fine mansion in Point Breeze, near Bordentown. Katzenbach became the proprietor of the Trenton House Inn, at that time one of the most well-known hotels in New Jersey.

Peter's son, Frank, graduated from Princeton University in 1867 and became a successful hardware merchant in Trenton. His son, Frank Jr., was twice elected mayor of Trenton and ran a close second in the Democratic gubernatorial election in 1907. He was appointed a justice of the New Jersey Supreme Court in 1920, holding that office until his death in 1929. Frank Sr.'s second son, Edward, served as attorney general of New Jersey from 1924 to 1929. Edward's wife, Marie Hilson Katzenbach, founded a school for the deaf in Trenton that is named after her and still exists.

Edward and Marie's children were as civic-minded as the rest of the family. Edward Jr., a Princeton professor, wrote speeches for President John F. Kennedy. His brother Nicholas, another Princeton graduate, is perhaps today the most famous of them all, having played a preeminent role in the civil rights movement of the 1960s, as deputy attorney general of the United States under Robert Kennedy, and then attorney general under President Lyndon Johnson.

Such were the distinguished individuals who spent time at Frank Sr.'s home in Spring Lake over the years. It was the perfect summer cottage for the Katzenbach family and their friends, being both modest and spectacular at the same time. It cost $4,075, excluding the cost of hardware, plumbing and other supplies, which presumably came from the Katzenbach hardware store in Trenton. A year after the house was completed, a barn was added, at a cost of $775.

The architect was H. E. Finch, whose design is a delightfully extreme example of the Queen Anne style. The house is like a case study for architectural students of the period—a dazzling display of pitched rooflines, stained glass windows, a conical tower with a witch's cap, turned spindles, fretwork, wraparound porches, scroll work in gable ends, and perhaps most wonderful of all, shingles applied in no less than nine different patterns. The front entrance is like the final punctuation of this architectural showcase—a massive Dutch door that came from a Katzenbach mansion in Trenton.

The house remained in the family for almost ninety years, when its second owners, Rosemary and Victor Rizzi of Princeton, New Jersey, purchased the property. It was in fine condition, "no doubt because it was used by a continuous line of the same family as a summer home for all those years," says Rosemary Rizzi. The new owners made a few necessary renovations, but continue to act as honorable caretakers of this old and much-loved holiday cottage, whose original family gave it its name and resonance in the history, not only of New Jersey, but of the United States of America.

"I USED TO ROMP AROUND A GREAT HOUSE IN THE PHILIPPINES ..."

One of the most magnificent mansions in a cluster of magnificence along First Avenue is known as the Kirkbride Cottage, at 100 Mercer Avenue. It has a long and complicated provenance. The land, like much of the real estate along the shore here, was owned by the Spring Lake Improvement Company, which sold it in 1878 to George C. Hulitt, who built the original house, perhaps as a speculation. Hulitt (or Hulet) was one of the original landowners of Spring Lake, and he built the first Spring Lake Railroad Station—one of those critical moments in the development of these shore communities—creating a vital link between Philadelphia and New York.

Hulitt sold the property to Frederick Anspach of Philadelphia, an engineer involved in the planning of Spring Lake Beach. In 1882 Anspach sold it to James Dougherty, and in 1892 Dougherty deeded it to Euletta Dougherty Kirkbride, presumably his daughter. Euletta's husband was Dr. M. Frank Kirkbride, an early specialist in mental health, called in those days an alienist. (Now we would call him a psychiatrist.) The Kirkbrides lived in Philadelphia and used the house as a summer cottage for many years.

The Kirkbride family continued to live in the house until 1936, when the last member, James. D. Kirkbride, died. The house was then abandoned for several years, and was boarded up, its fate uncertain. Rescue came in the form of Mr. and Mrs. Emory C. Smith, who bought the property in 1949 for themselves and their three children. The most miraculous aspect of this story is that because the house was uninhabited and boarded up for more than ten years, it remained untouched, both inside and out. One can imagine how new owners might have "spruced up" the interior and "cleaned up" the exterior, adding commercially made windows and screened-in porches or other modern touches that would have ruined the perfection of the house. The Smiths found their house almost exactly as the Kirkbrides had lived in it.

Betsy Smith, the Emory Smiths' daughter, recalled how her father had to climb through the window to get a look at the inside of the house before making the purchase. Imagine what he would have seen! The ceilings were ten feet high. There was a grand staircase made of quartered oak, with stained glass windows on the landings. There were two fireplaces and several cast-iron wall regulators that indicated early central heating, suggesting the family liked to stay on in their house after the summer temperatures had declined. Fine paneling

Even in the pantheon of Spring Lake Gilded Age mansions, this one has no equal. Known as the Kirkbride Cottage, it was built probably as a speculation house in the boom period of about 1878. After changing hands twice, it was deeded to the Kirkbride family in 1892.

and moldings decorated the rooms, made of chestnut, cherrywood, and oak, including folding cherrywood shutters on every window. The house had a billiard room, a game room, five bathrooms, and ten bedrooms, not including the servants' rooms, plus a large finished attic. There was a bell system for summoning the servants. Mr. Smith must certainly have gotten an eyeful when he went through that window.

In 1979 Ramon and Lourdes Cuasay, both doctors, bought the Kirkbride Cottage from the Smiths. Lourdes Cuasay had accepted a position at the Jersey Shore University Medical Center and the couple were looking to move from South Jersey. "The parent of one of my patients who grew up and still lived in Spring Lake described the town so vividly to us that we took a tour with her," she recalls, "and we fell in love with this house, which had been on the market for a long time because of its size and age.

"I used to romp around a great house in the Philippines called the Apacible Mansion. It

ABOVE *The shore-facing façade shows its intricate and brilliantly executed design of multi-level balconies, curvilinear porch lines, finely carved eaves, pediments, and balustrades. The unusual running-diamond fretwork door panels offer an amusing contrast to the rest of the architecture.*

RIGHT *When the Cuasays bought the house, it was salmon pink. Their much-pondered decision to change it to blue and white turns out to have been inspired, as the interplay of color and light makes apparent.*

The interior of the house has many original features, including the chestnut, cherrywood, and oak moldings, cherrywood shutters, and the fine cherrywood mantel in the front parlor decorated with Italian tiles.

was owned by my grand-uncle, who was a governor of the province at that time," Dr. Cuasay continues. "The woodwork, high ceilings, stairway, and glasswork of that place astounded me, and made such an impression that I always longed for a house like it." (The Apacible Mansion, now a museum, was featured in the book *Filipino Style*, by René Javellana.) "We also have a large family, so the Kirkbride Cottage is perfect for reunions." A final factor that persuaded Dr. Cuasay to buy the house was that Betsy Smith's birthday was the same as her own. "We connected immediately and are good friends to this day."

When the Cuasays bought the house it was painted dark salmon pink. The new owners repainted it yellow with a brown roof, and after ten years changed it to peach, blue, and white, "to match the colors of the sunset," Dr. Cuasay says. "A Victorian idea." After another ten years, they settled on the present palette of Harbor Blue and dark blue with white trim, "the color of the sky on a beautiful day."

Today, the Kirkbride Cottage remains one the finest examples of late Victorian architecture to be found anywhere. Its many rooflines, stories, multi-level balconies and balustrades, dormers, pediments, fretwork, shingle patterns, and timbering make it a dazzling showcase of architectural styles, all combining to create a marvelously harmonious impression. The exterior paintwork reflects the virtuosity of the architecture. Having lived through many different paint colors over the years, it carries its current shades of blue and white well, the palette enhancing the subtle details of each intricately fashioned façade.

Its state of preservation is equally impressive, considering the maintenance that is involved in such a complex weaving of wood and shingle, a combination of art and craftsmanship that has sustained more than one hundred years of weathering salt, wind, summers, and winters at the Jersey Shore.

The lovely stained glass windows are original to the house, as is the quartered oak staircase.

REQUIEM FOR A GOTHIC TREASURE

In 1878 in the *Historical and Biographical Atlas of the New Jersey Coast*, the authors published two pages of lithographs of five Spring Lake houses owned by W. C. Hamilton. This atlas, published by Woolman & Rose in Philadelphia, listed among other things yacht owners, county surveys, shipwrecks, birds and fishes of the region, with pictorial views of the houses and hotels in the major developing communities along the Jersey Shore.

It is not clear why William C. Hamilton's cottages were selected to appear in the Woolman & Rose atlas. One clue is that he was listed as a patron of the publication, as were many businesses and hoteliers, eager to publicize their properties and establishments to readers and potential summer residents. Mr. Hamilton's five cottages illustrated are all very handsome. Two of them have widow's walks and verandahs on two floors; two have half-timbering. But one is very different from the other four. Designed in the Gothic Revival style, it has a tower with a widow's walk, a steeply pitched gabled roof, first- and second-floor verandahs with balustrades, elegant pillars with fretwork (Carpenter Gothic) decoration, and windows with shutters.

Since the illustrations appeared in 1878, all five houses had obviously already been constructed by that time. Mr. Hamilton, a Philadelphian, bought the land on Ocean Avenue from the Spring Lake Improvement Company and built the cottages, presumably to sell or rent. He sold the Gothic cottage in 1882 to Paul Graff for the princely sum of $9,300. The fate of Hamilton's other four cottages is not known. In 1909 the Breakers Hotel burned down, and many of the neighboring cottages on or near Ocean Avenue were damaged, including Graff's cottage. Fortunately, none of its characteristic architectural features were destroyed, and the cottage, known as the Hamilton Cottage, became a well-known landmark on the Spring Lake scene.

Over the years, changes were made. A different porch was constructed, with a distinctive pediment; the second-floor verandah was covered; the ground-floor verandahs got a new, pitched roofline. But its essential charm remained, and the striking tower and gingerbread ornamentation offered an interesting contrast to the more familiar Queen Anne and Victorian houses that line Spring Lake's showcase First Avenue.

Its Gothic splendor survived until June 2004, when it was torn down.

ABOVE *This Gothic masterpiece, overlaid with Italianate influences, was built by William C. Hamilton, who built four other cottages in Spring Lake. The date is sometime before 1878, when lithographs of all five of Hamilton's houses appeared in the atlas of Woolman & Rose of Philadelphia.*

BELOW LEFT *The Hamilton Cottage, as it became known, was bought by Paul Graff in 1882 for $9,300—a princely sum in those days. What Graff was purchasing was a magnificent statement of early Spring Lake architecture.*

BELOW RIGHT *The fabulous turret, with Gothic windows, elaborate eaves, and irregular rooflines, reflected a passionate and carefree vision that could not possibly be recreated today. And it will not be. The Hamilton Cottage no longer exists. It remains only in the memory of Spring Lake and in photographs such as these.*

Bay Head

"THE ACCOUNT BOOKS TIED THE FAMILY
TO THE HISTORY OF THE HOUSE."

This is a story of one man's dedicated pursuit of history. Edward King is a BMW dealer in Freehold, New Jersey, whose passion is the preservation and restoration of old houses, including an eighteenth-century house and barn in Colts Neck. One day, reading the local newspaper, *The Ocean Star*, he saw a rather shabby Shingle house advertised for sale in Bay Head that immediately piqued his interest. Without hesitating, he put in a bid, and in the autumn of 2004, he and his wife, Marybeth, became the owners of 500 Main Avenue, Bay Head. Knowing it was old, but not yet informed about its history, Ed dug back into old archives, census reports, and other documents that might help him understand the long-distant past of his new home. What he learned surprised him considerably.

It turns out that 500 Main Avenue is one of the most important houses in Bay Head. It was built in about 1882 by David H. Mount Jr. and his wife, Annie. David Mount was one of the founders of the town of Bay Head, when he formed the Bayhead Land Company in 1874, along with his two brothers-in-law, Edward Howe and William Harris, both bankers in Princeton. (The dates are ambiguous. The date of the deed is 1874, but William Schoettle, in his book *Bay Head 1879–1911*, states that the company was incorporated in 1879.) At the time of the deed, Bayhead was one word, but when the sign first went up at the new railroad station in 1881, it read as two words—"Bay Head." A sign-painter's mistake became the town's new and permanent name. It was incorporated as such in 1886.

The Mount family had settled in New Jersey in the mid-1700s or earlier, and were making a successful business with plaster, wood, grist, and sawmills along the Millstone River in Montgomery Township, Somerset County. Going back to early censuses, Ed King found the Mounts listed in the 1860, 1870, and 1880 censuses of Rocky Hill, showing the family as both being enormously wealthy and running an extensive household. David Jr. was

FACING One of the most important houses in Bay Head, 500 Main Avenue, was built in about 1882 for David H. Mount Jr., one of the founders of the town. Its history has many layers, yet the house has survived almost untouched for well over one hundred years.

79

described in the 1880 census as living next door to his father with a wife, Annie, and a son, Thomas.

Continuing to prosper, the entrepreneurial Mounts evidently decided to regard Bay Head as a valuable investment. In 1889 David H. Mount Jr. was not only living at 500 Main Avenue with his family, but was now mayor of the town, a position he held until 1890. The Mounts soon owned several other properties in the developing town, including two Stick-style houses on Howe Street, just west of Main Avenue, two more Stick-style houses on Lake Street, and one on the beach. All six Mount houses are still in existence.

They evidently spent summers there well into the twentieth century. According to the 1930 census (which Ed King studied during his research on the history of the house), David Mount, aged forty-seven, and Thomas Mount, aged forty-nine, were both living at 500 Main Avenue. Both brothers are listed as married. Thomas is described as an electrical engineer; his brother, "proprietor." The value of the house is listed as seven thousand dollars.

Having helped establish the community of Bay Head, the Mounts became some of the most highly regarded citizens in the town, involved in sailing, tennis, and the Bay Head Yacht Club. Their name is still very well known here and remembered by many old-timers. Thomas Mount's son, Tom Jr., kept the house in the family until 2004, when Ed and Marybeth King purchased the property. Little did they know that what they were about to embark on was to become a long and intricate detective story.

As might be imagined after so long in only one family's hands, the interior was in sore need of help. There were only two full baths (one with an old claw-and-ball-foot bathtub), and the interior moldings and plasterwork needed major repair, as did the plumbing and electricity. There seemed to be no evidence of the original kitchen, which was probably in the cellar. But the pine and hardwood floors had survived well, along with some fine details, such as the staircase banister's three handsome newel posts. The Kings consider the restoration of the inside of the house just as important as the outside. "My wife is in charge of the interior, and I concentrate on the exterior," Ed says.

The exterior of the house provided Ed and Marybeth King with their most complex challenges. Uncovering the history of the Mount family was just the beginning of the adventure of their impulsive acquisition. While exploring the house, they stumbled upon an unexpected trove of documents abandoned by the former owners. This kind of material is the gold from which biographers forge their subjects' lives, and with which Ed was able to recreate the original architecture of the house and its distinguished heritage.

In the attic of 500 Main Avenue, he found a notebook belonging to David H. Mount Jr., M.D., dated 1888, in which the writer describes treatments for the insane. (It seems David Mount was not only a real estate investor but also a doctor.) Ed also found old photographs and a pile of unframed maps, depicting the town of Bay Head in 1883. In the attic there was also an early-nineteenth-century chair, with stenciled decoration, clearly an heirloom from the original owners.

But his most important discovery came in a more unexpected place. In a closet on the

second floor, he found three account books. Dated 1879, they were from the Mounts' mills in Rocky Hill, New Jersey. This clue led Ed to the Mounts' original home in New Jersey. "The account books tied the family to the history of the house," he says. "They were the key to my research."

These random documents also helped him visualize the original look of 500 Main Avenue. At an exhibit at the Bay Head Historical Society's Loveland House Museum, he discovered a postcard of Bay Head, dated roughly 1900, showing Main Avenue as a dirt road, with several houses built along it. One of them is the Mount house. It looks in the picture as though it has new shingle siding. But Ed warns that in those days postcards were hand-colored and the shingles might be an artistic flourish. However, the "new" Shingle-style architecture was clearly visible on the house, so it is most likely that the house had been sided with Jersey white cedar shingles.

Ed was almost certain that the original façade was clapboard. He found remnants of the

It is thought by owners Ed and Marybeth King, whose delving into the house's past is worthy of Sherlock Holmes, that the shingles on the façade were an early replacement for clapboard.

The original architecture of the house turns out to have been Stick style. Today its sturdy shingles, pedimented portico, arched columns, and ornamented eaves make it a much-loved landmark of Bay Head.

original clapboard under the porch, painted blue-green. This was thought to be the original color until more recently, when some wall-covering was ripped off the exterior, revealing the clapboard painted a blood-red color. Shingles must have been applied later, most likely soon before the postcard was made, and they are retained up to today.

On closer study of the postcard, Ed saw something else that took him by surprise. The top of the house appeared to have a small steeple like a witch's hat peeking over the roofline of the other houses. No steeple existed by the time the Kings bought the house. Was this another trick of the old postcard-maker?

It seemed as though these questions would never be answered. But the house had not finished revealing its astonishing secrets. In an extraordinary later revelation, a workman in the attic found one more invaluable treasure—an authentic 1880s photograph, much faded

and in poor condition, of the original house. Not only was the façade clapboard, as the Kings suspected, but the steeple was also in place, topping a small bay that projected over the second floor. Eureka!

The Kings had already deduced much of what the photograph confirmed: that the house had a wood shingle roof, for instance. There was a remnant of lathe in the attic. Years later, Ed explains, asphalt roofing was installed—a popular innovation in roof construction introduced along the Jersey Shore as a preventive against the most common danger, fire. Ed plans to replace the asphalt with Jersey cedar shingles. Although the exterior of the house was built with clapboard, it has been shingled since the 1900s, and Ed has decided to re-shingle it, rather than revert to the original clapboard. "Shingles are considered lower maintenance," he says. "We shall use Jersey white cedar, as on the roof."

The photograph also confirmed that the house originally had movable louvered shutters with cast-iron hinges. An original pair of shutters exists in the cellar, and there are pintles, or pivot pins for hinges, still visible on several window frames. Ed intends to restore the windows and shutters to their appearance as first installed in 1880.

The photograph revealed something else entirely unexpected: the architecture of the house was originally Stick style, with front porch columns supported by diagonal braces, a first-floor balustrade and porch in the same style, shutters at the windows, and an entrance on the north side, rather than angled to the street as it is now.

While the discovery of this invaluable photograph of the original house was enormously exciting to architectural scholars and history aficionados, it created one outsized challenge for the new—stunned—owners. Should the Kings restore the house to its original Stick-style appearance? That would mean replacing the arched porch with square openings and diagonal posts, changing the balustrades, repositioning the entrance, and restoring the steeple—an enormous task. It would mean, in effect, completely rebuilding the house.

The Kings finally decided against restoring the house back to its appearance as shown in the photo found in the attic. "We felt that the design that was updated by the remodelers around 1900 was so connected to the other structures in Bay Head that restoring the house to the 1880s Stick style would have been like building a brand-new house. Certainly nobody

ABOVE LEFT *Ed King's meticulous restoration of the house revealed original paneling, paint colors, and glass, which he is taking care to preserve.*
ABOVE RIGHT *The house originally had movable louvered shutters with cast-iron hinges, some of which are still visible on a few of the window frames.*

now living remembers the original house. Also, the corner steps and porch have become such a familiar sight to those driving south on Main Avenue that to change the house would be more a loss for the environment than a gain."

There are other arguments in favor of the Kings' decision. Stick-style architecture, while very popular from 1850 to 1890, turned out to have a fragility that was not very practical for a house on the shore. That perhaps is the reason that at only about twenty years into the house's history, the Stick style was subsumed into more sturdy local vernacular traditions. Should the Kings be faithful to history to the extent of endangering the survival of the house?

The steeple is a case in point. According to the last owner, David H. Mount Jr.'s grandson Tom Mount (now aged ninety-six), the steeple blew off in a storm. In other words, it is not a stable architectural form in this wind-tossed environment. Moreover, as Ed King points out, "we would have to go for a height variance, and would the planning board grant a height variance to enable us to make the house historically correct?" Probably not.

Michael Calafati, of Historic Building Architects, is working with the Kings on the restoration of 500 Main Avenue. "These unusual dilemmas," he observes, "are momentous for those concerned about architectural history and restoration. . . . The wonderful thing about this house is that it is so untouched over so many years. Yet now we must make sure that our steps are measured and carefully thought out, so that we do not disturb the character of the house. Of course, after one hundred years materials get worn out, and we must replace them, but we must replace them with building materials and assemblies that are in harmony with the original concept."

Fortunately, the Kings are remarkably well attuned to the situation in which they find themselves. Ed's knowledge of early building practices, and his ability to do the necessary research, along with his wife's design talents and the expert help of Michael Calafati, are giving 500 Main Avenue a chance to embark on a new life that carefully reflects the old. In doing so, the Kings have come up with a wonderfully vivid picture of the early days of the house and of those first settlers who turned the town of Bay Head into the summer paradise that it is today. 🐎

"IT IS PERFECTLY FREE FROM MALARIA."

When David H. Mount Jr. and his brothers-in-law invested in Bay Head, the land consisted of sand dunes on the ocean side and a bay to the west surrounded by bayberry, beach-plum bushes, and marshes; yet it was soon clear that this was desirable property. The Philadelphia and Long Beach Railroad opened for business in Bay Head in 1881, its final destination, and with it the town became a magnet for Philadelphians who wished to escape urban life in the summertime, when the city became too hot and humid for comfort.

Two of the earliest settlers were professors from what was then called the College of New Jersey, now Princeton University. Dr. H. C. Cameron, whose house was at the north end of the town, taught ancient Greek, and his colleague Professor Karge, who resided at the southernmost limit of the town, taught Continental languages and literature. An early boardwalk ran between their houses, which was later extended as the town pushed farther north and south. The Karges' closest neighbor was the Life-Saving Station, which had been originally built in 1871. Beyond this cluster of buildings, the town ended abruptly, giving way to dunes and ocean and stunning views towards Barnegat Bay.

In 1881 the first hotel, the Bellevue, was built, to provide lodging near the station for those discovering the convenience of taking the train to the shore. Its competition, the Grenville, a large Queen Anne–style structure, was built at about the same time as The Bluffs, which went up in 1891. Another hotel, the Ocean View House, quickly followed. (Only the Grenville still stands.)

The Bluffs became the center of social life during the early twentieth century. "Euchre parties, Germans, concerts, amateur theatricals, Shakespearean recitals, tableaux, hops under the direction of the orchestra leader, Professor J. H. Peterman, kept this hotel a beehive of activity," William Schoettle writes in *Bay Head 1879–1911*. The Ocean View House was also popular. "The bedrooms are furnished in the most comfortable manner, best springs and hair mattresses," the hotel's brochure declared. "Most of the rooms open out on the broad piazza. . . . We have a magnificent white sand beach, and there is no dreaded undertow." The hotel also assured guests that Bay Head "is considered one of the most healthy places on the coast, and is the summer home of many New York and Philadelphian physicians. It is perfectly free from malaria, and those suffering from rose or hay fever soon find relief, and its quiet, restful and health-giving air is an excellent tonic for sufferers from nervous troubles."

The classic Shingle façade, with gambrel roof and dormers, is unchanged since its construction in 1902. The long, east-facing porch, destroyed by a hurricane in the 1950s, was returned to its former glory by the Fortenbaughs in the 1980s.

Health was clearly one of the issues that occupied the minds of visiting holidaymakers to the shore in those years. One of Bay Head's early settlers was a distinguished New York physician, William H. Katzenbach. According to William Schoettle, the doctor was a no-nonsense diagnostician. He would describe in brisk terms the sickness of vacationing children to their worried parents as "the three Cs: too much cantaloupe, too much corn and too much cold water."

Such reassurances, as well as other more practical factors like convenience and natural beauty, ensured the town's success, and many new cottages were built, both north and south on the oceanfront and inland towards the bay. The community rapidly expanded with churches, a school, and the Yacht Club.

Today, much of that old charm remains. Fires, hurricanes, and fierce northeast storms have taken their toll, but the atmosphere is still that of a small town. Bay Head is unusual in that most beachfront homeowners have good title to mean-high water. That means they largely own the beach, which for years was closed to the general public. Today that has changed and beach badges are now available to all. Until as recently as 1962, a boardwalk ran along the beach from north to south, past the houses and hotels of what is now East Avenue and ending at Johnson Street. A northeast storm in March 1962 took out most of the board-walk, and also did serious damage to oceanfront properties. That prompted a group of prominent Bay Head residents to bring in rocks and build both a stone wall fifteen feet into the sand and a string of groins or jetties that protrude into the sea. Thanks to these groins, Bay Head now has twice as much beach as it had before 1962.

Sometimes Bay Head is compared to Nantucket or Martha's Vineyard because of its fine old shingle and clapboard houses and its success in fending off the fast-food or souvenir shops that the shore invariably attracts. The town is a center for sailing, tennis, and other summer sports. The Bay Head Yacht Club, dating back to 1888, is well known among sailors throughout the East Coast and beyond.

Main, East, and Bridge Avenues are modern versions of the three original gravel streets that once dominated the town. One of the typical Shingle-built houses that were fashion-able in the town's early history is 617 East Avenue. It is thought to have been part of a prop-erty called "Bluff," since it is only a hundred yards from the splendid eponymous hotel that stood there until 1996, when it was demolished. The house is owned by William and Constance Fortenbaugh. Bill's parents bought it in 1943 from the Pendletons, who in turn bought it from the first owners, probably in the 1920s or before.

The Fortenbaughs believe that the house was built in 1902. On the red brick mantel in the living room, the date "September 20, 1903" can be read, along with the names "Mc-Neal" and "Willie." This inscription, accompanied by a small line, measures the height of two of the original owners' children. Several other lines can also be made out, moving higher up the wall as the children grew.

The front façade of 617 East Avenue, like its neighbors, faces east towards the beach. Thus

On wind-free days, a corner of the porch offers a tranquil spot for watching the ocean and dunes.

A path from this Bay Head house through the dunes to the sunlit ocean reassures the beach-lover that the pristine beauty of the Jersey Shore will never lose its magic.

it could be admired by the holidaymakers passing by on the boardwalk during their promenades. This decision caused major problems over the years, since most of the worst storms sweeping up the coast paid scant respect to the beauty of the local architecture. A hurricane in the 1950s took off the front porch of the house, which stayed off until Bill and Connie put it back on in the 1980s. They rebuilt it in long-lasting cedar that needs no paint. Bill expects the porch to outlive his children—unless a hurricane takes it out again. While today some may question the advantage of having an east-facing porch, Bill points out that although the east side of the house has to bear the brunt of the weather, it is cooled by the sea breeze—an important factor in houses without air conditioning.

During the second ownership of the house, the south-facing second-floor verandah was closed in, an infamy in terms of its architecture, but a practical decision that has provided the current inhabitants with a small, pretty conservatory that offers a fine view of the ocean. Another small adjustment was the transformation of a bay window off the dining room into a door. In the old days, the owners and their friends came in through the front of the house—that is, the porch door on the beachfront. The help used the basement entry. Before the Fortenbaughs acquired the house, someone (perhaps the Pendletons) decided that there was

The second-floor verandah was closed in during the tenure of the second owners of the house—bad news for architectural
purists, but good news for those who now enjoy an excellent view of the ocean from this sunny conservatory and sitting room.

Inside this fine old cottage, the rooms retain a strong sense of the past. The dining room ceiling and walls are as old as the house, offering a comfortable context for the owners' inherited furniture and collections.

The living room maintains its original character, with the red brick fireplace, grass-cloth wall coverings, and Southern pine wood trim. The sense of history is enhanced by family furniture, heirlooms, and sailing mementos.

The original staircase was built to last. Arts and Crafts furnishings and lamps give period authenticity to the interior of the house.

need for a third entrance. It was difficult in stormy weather for people to struggle round the house to reach the door on the front porch. A side entrance was desirable, even if it meant entering through the dining room.

As for the interior decoration, almost everything is original. Bill's mother had most of the wood painted blue, but he had it stripped. His mother also removed the grass-cloth that covered the living room walls. Bill has had it replaced. The wood is mostly Southern pine, with wainscoting, beams, and other decorative moldings. The living-room fireplace with its soft red brick is a striking feature. The Fortenbaughs know they could never paint it or alter it because of the original names and dates written on the brick—precious archaeology. The furniture, mostly in the Arts and Crafts style of the early 1900s, remains unchanged.

Bill Fortenbaugh, following the sturdy tradition of his Bay Head predecessors, is a professor of classics at Rutgers University, and also a keen sailor, as the Yacht Club memorabilia displayed in many of the rooms indicates. He and his wife use the house year-round, and for all family events. Keeping up such a magnificent old place is a challenge. They have just re-shingled the back of the house. "It is supposed to last forty years but not this close to the ocean," he remarks ruefully. Yet their care and attention, as well as a fondness for tradition, have ensured that this house continues to connect with a past that in many other ways has been long overtaken. "The trend is to tear down places like this," Bill says. "Or to 'modernize' them, by enclosing porches and then installing air-conditioning. None of that makes sense to me." Luckily for lovers of history, continuity, and early American architecture, the Fortenbaughs are making a stand that will be appreciated for years to come—as long as Mother Nature cooperates. 🐚

This handsome bay window is one of a pair on the south side of the house. The second one was turned into a door to create an entrance off the dining room.

Mantoloking

"[IT] WAS SURROUNDED BY SALT HAY MARSHES,
HARVESTED FOR THE LIVESTOCK."

Mantoloking, like many Jersey Shore towns, has lost several of its historic houses, but William and Julie Dunbar own one of the oldest in the region. It was built in 1910 for Orton Goodwin Dale, an engineer for the Pennsylvania Railroad, in a splendid location on what was then called High Hill Point, far out on the tip of the lagoon. (It is now 225 Channel Lane.) O. G. Dale (as he was known) moved to High Hill Point from Bay Head, where he had been a very popular member of the Bay Head Yacht Club and won several championships with his boat, the *Arran*. It was said that when O.G. moved to Mantoloking, it must have taken a separate carload to move the sailing trophies he had won.

The builder of O.G.'s new house was Harry L. Johnson, and his contract for the construction still exists. In consideration of its grandeur, the house cost the owner $3,550 to construct, roughly $159,000 in today's terms—very good value for those days. (Blairsden, in central New Jersey, built a little prior to the Dale house, while admittedly on a far grander scale, would cost in today's money $25 million.)

Its architecture is typical of the region at the turn of the century—a clapboard façade with shutters, large porches, two chimneys, and a gambrel roof. In 1911, as a portent of the already budding development of the town (mostly by Philadelphians), O. G. Dale asked his colleagues at the Pennsylvania Railroad to build a railroad crossing for his driveway leading from Ocean Avenue to the house. (That driveway is now Bergen Avenue.) Its lonely magnificence may be seen in a photograph taken at the time. According to the Dunbars, "the Dale house was the only house on High Hill Point and was surrounded by salt hay marshes, harvested for the livestock."

Moving a house from one location to another was—and remains—an American custom much remarked on by Europeans, who cannot imagine doing such a thing. In 1930, after the

FACING *This is one of the oldest houses in Mantoloking. Built in 1910 for O. G. Dale, an engineer for the Pennsylvania Railroad, it still has the original shingles, gambrel roof, and shutters. It has had only three owners. The porches have been enclosed and new roofs and windows installed, but otherwise it retains its historic character.*

surrounding lagoons were dredged, O. G. Dale moved his house to its present location at 937 Lagoon Lane. The procedure seems to have gone without a hitch. Some time later, Ruth Hurley bought the house from Mr. Dale, who, having become afraid that a wooden house would burn down, decided he wanted to live in one built of brick. (Ironically, his life ended in the opposite way from how he had imagined it. One winter he fell through the ice and drowned.) Mrs. Hurley sold it to the present owners in 1978.

Thus the house has only had three owners, which explains in part how it remains so very faithful to its original form. Although it has not surprisingly been subject to pressures of modern living, its wooden framework is original, and the roofline, shingles, and shutters remain the same. The porches have been enclosed, and windows expanded. There is a new roof, and one chimney instead of two, after one of them rotted. Bathrooms were modernized. Storm windows were installed. The most amusing change to the exterior did not involve the house at all, but the front walk, which came with the building, in the form of wooden duckboards. The Dunbars replaced the duckboards with brick.

Little of the interior has been altered. The bedrooms are quite small, off a main corridor, as in the original floor plan. The floors, door frames, and moldings are all original to the house. This remarkable feat of preservation deserves the gratitude of both the house and those who care about architectural history. The Dunbars, who live here year-round, are deeply aware of their responsibility to this almost century-old masterpiece, and preserve all the documentation still extant about its past, including bills of sale and other paperwork from the original construction. It may not come as a surprise that Bill Dunbar is mayor of Mantoloking, a suitable caretaker, with his wife, Julie, of this historic house.

A SMALL FRENCH CHATEAU IN THE NEW WORLD

On the beach at the point where Bay Head's town line meets the northern end of Mantoloking sits a Normandy-style house built in 1925. Nestled in high dunes planted with beach plums, bayberry bushes, and black pines, the house can barely be seen from either the beach or the street. Its gabled and dormered cedar-shake roof tops cream-colored stucco walls with olive-green trim. Its architectural style, elevation, and natural landscaping make it a striking contrast to traditional Jersey Shore houses. One could believe it is a small French chateau transplanted across the ocean!

The house was designed by Arthur Dillon (1870–1937), a well-known New York architect. His previous work was influenced by the training he had received at the Ecole des Beaux-Arts in Paris, where many of his American contemporaries, such as Richard Morris Hunt and both partners of Carrère & Hastings, had also studied. The French influence is reflected in Dillon's French Revival design for the St. Louis Club in Missouri, built in 1900, that still stands on the St. Louis University campus.

In 1912, as part of a new partnership, Dillon, McClellan and Beadle, he designed the Champlain Memorial on Lake Champlain in New York. Originally incorporated into a lighthouse, the building is a small neo-classical temple with French architectural details reminiscent of the hunting lodge at Fontainebleau. Dillon was also the architect for the public library in South Orange, New Jersey, built in 1925.

In 1925, Dillon was commissioned by Mrs. B. B. Schneider Jr. to plan a summer house for her on the Mantoloking beach. The original blueprints and artist's sketches still exist and are in the possession of Mrs. D. C. Franklin, the home's second and current owner. Mrs. Franklin, who bought the property in 1955, also has a collection of old photographs of the area. From these invaluable archives it is possible to trace much of the history of the house.

They confirm that the house has changed little since it was built. The stucco has lasted well and the exterior walls and trim are still painted in the same colors as the original. The floor plan was changed slightly when Mrs. Franklin expanded the kitchen wing in 1994, and when the south-facing porch was enclosed to make it usable year-round. A separate garage that borders the street and matches the design of the main house was part of Dillon's original plan. It was spacious enough for Mrs. Schneider's chauffeur to sleep in and was equipped with a basin and toilet that have since been removed.

FACING *Nestled in the dunes amidst a
flourish of bayberry, beach plum, and
evergreens, this cottage has the allure of a
French chateau, with its gables, dormers,
steep rooflines, and brick chimney.*

ABOVE *The cream-colored stucco walls, here
part of a south-facing porch that was closed in
by the present owner, Mrs. D. C. Franklin, also
seem European in flavor. A simple path and
fence, planted with salt-hardy native shrubs,
lead past the side of the house to the beach.*

RIGHT *The ocean side of the house has
a simple, split-level deck, where once
there had been nothing but sand.*

Improvements to the house and property over the years have been done in the French style, with loyalty to Dillon's details. Three sets of French doors that opened onto the beach under a colonnade spanning the eastern side of the house have been replaced by identically sized casement windows, double-glazed and energy-efficient. Central air conditioning has replaced window awnings to cool the house, with the equipment well hidden behind plantings under a large holly tree. Wooden decking around the perimeter of the house protects the dunes while providing outdoor living space.

Mrs. Franklin's commitment to preserving the architectural integrity of the house is evident in the beautiful French details of the interior space. The large living room features an original stucco-and-brick chimneypiece. The ceiling has exposed pickled cypress beams and the floors are pine, stained in a rich, dark brown. Mrs. Franklin's excellent choice of furniture and decoration has made this room a fine example of French Country style. Throughout the house the stucco walls are white, the floors are dark, and the doors and windows are pickled in gray. When a door or wood trim has been replaced it has been meticulously painted in trompe l'oeil to match the original.

The same devotion to detail and esthetics inspired Mrs. Franklin to create a garden full of hardy, indigenous plants and to landscape her property with trees and dune grasses to beautifully wild effect. Although the dunes have shifted over the years, she has secured them with bayberry, *rosa rugosa*, black pines, sea grasses, and Russian olives. Where the pebbled driveway splits the dune, it curves behind the higher bank to hide any parked cars. A years-long battle with poison ivy, which thrived atop the bayberry bushes, was eventually won, and baby pink roses were planted randomly in its place. An olive-green picket fence lines the street side of this property, keeping in check the naturally planted and slowly shifting dunes. A small gate opens onto a narrow path leading to the well-hidden front door of a house that stands as an artful, surviving testament to the talents of Arthur Dillon and to the devotion and good taste of its owner.

"WHEN WE FOUND THIS PLACE IN THE LATE 1980S, IT WAS TOTALLY NEGLECTED."

In a small, tightly planned community like Mantoloking, making a garden creates a special challenge. Mostly it's a question of space. Mark and Susan Hawkings have come up with a brilliant way of tricking their 75-by-250-foot property into a surprising and widely varied garden landscape. By contrasting light and shade, greenery and bright color, and by using winding paths to create mystery, they have produced a delightful secret garden along the banks of a Mantoloking lagoon.

"We bought the house because it's hard to find a decent piece of property on the shore with a garden," explains Mark Hawkings, an Englishman who was evacuated in World War II to the United States. (He was on the last evacuee boat to cross the Atlantic before it became too dangerous.) After the war he returned to Britain and was commissioned in the Grenadier Guards. He came back to the United States to accept a job offer and has stayed ever since.

The entrance to the house is paved with patterned tiles, leading the eye through a wooden gateway, draped in blue spruce and holly, towards the lagoon. In front are crescent-shaped beds filled with brightly colored zinnias and other annuals.

Perhaps because of his English blood, he was always drawn to gardening. He and his wife, Susan, had owned a small garden in Bay Head before moving to this house in Mantoloking because of its potentially bigger garden, when their children were grown. They looked for a long time. "When we found this place in the late 1980s, it was totally neglected."

"Neglected" is not too strong a word. The garden was all gravel. There were a few sad-looking trees. The hedges had not been cut for ten years. "Neighbors laughed at our folly," recalls Mark Hawkings. "But we took the plunge. The first thing I did was start to prune. It was like pruning the Amazon!"

The counterpunch to this depressing prospect was that the first owner, who bought the land after World War II, had covered the whole property with topsoil, so that even now the ground is one foot higher than that of their neighbors. "We aren't very popular in a flood!" Mark laughs.

This gift of good soil has reaped huge rewards for Mark and Susan. They completely redesigned the entryway. Espaliered cotoneaster climbs up the front fence overlooking an

annual border, making an inviting entrance. A brick path leads the visitor through wooden gates, punctuated on each side by blue spruce and holly. Inside, a winding path leads past a shadowy arbor on the left, where an unusually shaped silver poplar, very old and covered with ivy, seems to be lying down on the grass like a crouching dragon. Through the arbor is a small green garden with shrubs and shade plants.

The path takes a turn towards the house, where a newly designed raised bed is filled with annuals, such as Wave petunias and verbena, giving lots of color to this part of the property. A young magnolia dominates the space. It replaces a blue spruce that fell onto the house in a storm. A newly installed drywall frames this cheerful landscape. The roses by the wall have an interesting history—they were sent from Harry & David as a gift to the Hawkingses' daughter. On a whim, Mark planted them, and they have grown into marvelously healthy bushes.

At the front of the house a lawn runs down to the lagoon, where boats bob and ducks swim. Along the lagoon's edge, Mark and Susan planted annual dahlias, zinnias, and verbena. Lilacs and a Japanese silverball mark the perimeter of the garden, along with tomatoes in season. The splendid Friesian cow "swam across to us," as Mark put it, from a recently deceased neighbor.

While the garden looks now as though it has been here for many years, Mark, like most true gardeners, is constantly changing the design and replanting. He continues to discover paths that once threaded through the property, and nurtures old shrubs that he has uncovered and that still have life in them. He says it keeps him young. "He does everything," says his wife. "I just water." 🐚

ABOVE *In the shady back garden to the left of the house lies a strangely shaped ivy-covered creature that is in fact a silver poplar, sinking to its knees with old age.*
FACING *In twenty or so years, the garden, only 75 by 250 feet in size, has been transformed by its owners from a gravel graveyard into a riot of flowers, paths, shrubs, and trees. This recently installed drywall is the foundation for roses that were a gift to their daughter.*

Lavallette

A HOUSE WITH A PAST

Lavallette, like Brigantine, its cousin to the south, was a late developer. Until the late 1800s not much was happening, although, as T. E. Rose wrote at the time, "the situation is dry and the air is pure and wholesome; even that which blows from the land must cross between two and three miles of salt water before it reaches the beach."

One of its problems was similar to that of other shore towns in their infancy—it was difficult to get to. You had to take a train to Toms River and then change to a steamer for the seven-mile trip to Lavallette. In 1883 the Pennsylvania Railroad added a spur from Toms River over a bridge to Seaside Park, thus opening up the communities from Lavallette to Mantoloking, and development quickly followed.

Lavallette was named in honor of Rear Admiral Elie A. F. La Vallette. Of French origin, Lavallette (he Anglicized the name in 1830) fought in the Battle of Champlain during the War of 1812, and was involved in many other skirmishes. President Lincoln promoted him to Rear Admiral on July 30, 1862, and three months later the distinguished sailor died at the Philadelphia Navy Yard. His son, A. T. Lavallette, was secretary of the Barnegat Land Improvement Company. Perhaps his influence on Jersey Shore property prompted the town's developers to choose Lavallette City as its name.

By the early 1900s, Lavallette was ready for paved roads, businesses, churches, a summer population, and some very striking architecture. In 1917 a house was built on Brown Avenue that was the tallest structure for almost two miles. Its height, plus its position on the highest ground in town, were found invaluable for shipping, and the house was used as a marker on navigational charts for ships entering and departing from New York Harbor. But perhaps its most famous role was as a distant player in one of the most scandalous murders in the history of New Jersey.

FACING *The silhouetted balustrade makes a particularly striking note on the second-floor balcony, elegantly underlining the view of the ocean.*

The porch of this wood-framed mansion, dating from 1917, wraps around the east and south sides of the house. Supported by elegant square columns, it provides an excellent place for the children of the house to take a break from the beach.

The house was built by William Perry of Boston for Henry Stevens, a professional sharp-shooter and heir to part of the Johnson & Johnson fortune. Money seems to have been no object in funding his lavish and very solidly built oceanfront home, which required the talents of a large number of local craftsmen and construction workers. It is a wood-frame, three-story structure on a concrete foundation, with cedar-shake siding, a gambrel roof, and three dormers. A porch with a balcony above it runs the length of the east and south sides of the house, supported by simple wooden columns. The second-floor balcony is dominated by a balustrade designed in the Chinese Chippendale style. An entrance to the south side of the balcony is enhanced by a charming wood-framed portico that conveys the feeling of a tent, also with Chinese Chippendale decoration. Originally there was a greenhouse on the north side, connected to the main house by a breezeway.

Already a notable addition to the landscape of Lavallette, the Stevens House acquired even more notoriety in 1926, when Henry Stevens appeared as one of four defendants in the

The south-facing façade shows its architectural merit, with cedar-shake siding, a full-length porch, Chinese Chippendale balustrades on the second floor, and three pedimented dormers jutting out of a gambrel roof.

The unusual and extremely elegant Chinese Chippendale portico on the second floor indicates that the house belonged to an important person in town.

trial of what came to be called the Hall–Mills murders. The crime was particularly juicy. The victims were the Reverend Edward Wheeler Mills, pastor of the Church of St. John the Evangelist in New Brunswick, and Mrs. Eleanor Hall, who sang in the choir. (Pastor Mills was married to a Johnson & Johnson heiress. Mrs. Hall's husband was a janitor.) The couple was found dead under a crab-apple tree on a farm in Franklin Township in the early morning of September 15, 1922. Both had been shot, and Mrs. Hall's throat had been slashed. The minister's business card and love letters to him from Mrs. Hall were found scattered over the bodies.

The connection of this sensational event to the Stevens House was tenuous but thrilling. The Reverend Hall's widow, Frances, was a Stevens, and she and her two brothers, Henry and William, along with a cousin, were accused of the murders. Henry's alibi was that he was at his house in Lavallette at the time, fishing. (Since Stevens was a local councilman, the mayor of Lavallette felt it incumbent upon himself to pass a resolution supporting his colleague's alibi.)

The four suspects were acquitted for lack of evidence, and to this day nobody has been found guilty of the crime. Various efforts were made to call a retrial, but in the end New Jersey Attorney General Edward Katzenbach (whose family lived a little way up the shore to the north; see p. 88), washed his hands of the affair. (In the 1990s civil-rights lawyer William Kunstler wrote a book about the case and came to the conclusion it had been a Ku Klux Klan killing. Not many people agreed with him.)

In 1972 the house was purchased from the Stevens family by Norman Berson, whose father had helped build it. The house was in poor shape by this time, and the new owners took out a stairway, built a new kitchen, and restored the exterior to its original beauty. In 1985 Mr. and Mrs. Clemente J. Liccardi, who had lived for fifty-four years on Brown Avenue, decided they would like to move closer to the ocean and bought the house, which was again on the market. They repainted it. "It was brown," explains Mrs. Liccardi, "and was known as the Brown house on Brown Avenue." They also turned the greenhouse into a sunroom, and now they live in it all summer long with their children and grandchildren. "There are nineteen people here every weekend," Mrs. Liccardi says.

The Stevens House has withstood storms, floods, and neglect, but it has never escaped its link to "the most famous unsolved crime of the century," as newspapers described it. Mrs. Liccardi tells of children who would run past it along the beach as fast as they could, believing it was haunted. Today, it has a happier role as a beachfront paradise for a host of children and grandchildren, whose thoughts are on far more important summer matters than a pair of murders that took place in another part of the state in a long-ago time.

Barnegat Light

"CAPT. BEN RANDOLPH KNOCKED OVERBOARD AND DROWNED."

The origins of the history of Long Beach Island can be traced to its northernmost tip, where the Barnegat Lighthouse towers 165 feet above the narrow strip of land stretching eighteen miles southwards beneath it. The northern waters of Long Beach Island were discovered by Henry Hudson in 1609, who called them Barnegat Inlet. (The name is a derivation of the Dutch word *Barende-gat*, meaning "Breakers' Inlet.") The lighthouse was built in 1834, an invaluable guide to the treacherous currents, breakers, and shoals of the rocky Atlantic coast, where countless sailors and fishermen risked their lives in their precarious vessels. Long Beach Island was inaccessible except by boat until the railway connection was built in 1885, and even that was a limited entry until the Manahawkin Bridge was built in 1914.

Thus the island's beauties remained a secret except to a very few local fishermen, whalers, and farmers until, like the rest of the Jersey Shore, it was discovered by the urban flocks looking for a summer resort. Even after the bridge was built, the northern end was not quickly settled, since it was the farthest away from the lines of communication. Roads took their time in reaching Barnegat City, as it was then called.

Life at the tip of the island was exciting. In one two-year period in the 1840s, it is said that 122 vessels were wrecked off the island. Even with "Old Barney" doing its best to warn intrepid sailors of the dangers, early regional writings are filled with electrifying reports of shipwrecks and fishing adventures witnessed by the awestruck locals: "The night of Oct. 30, 1890, the Spanish Steamer Viscaya and the four-masted schooner Cornelius Hargraves collided 8 miles off Barnegat Light. Of the 17 passengers, not one escaped . . ."; "Nov. 21, 1890, schooner Frances Hallock in collision with another schooner off Barnegat. Capt. Ben Randolph knocked overboard and drowned . . ."

FACING *While Barnegat Light has always been a community of working fishermen, some members of the town made good money a century or more ago and built splendid houses like this one, a grand display of Stick-style architecture of the late 1800s, with shingles, gables, bracketed arches, and dormers.*

This part of Long Beach Island is still suffused with the sense of fishing traditions. The Viking Village on the inlet was originally built by a group of Norwegian fishermen who knew that whatever the risks, fishing in Barnegat Bay would likely be extremely profitable. And so it turned out to be. Commercial fishing is still a dominant feature of Barnegat Light, with families who settled here in the nineteenth century still running some of the biggest long-line fleets on the East Coast, shipping millions of pounds of fish a year.

Fishermen could grow rich here, and by the looks of their houses, they enthusiastically spent their money on real estate. A few of the major houses that were built before the end of the nineteenth century still stand, particularly on 12th Street, a charmingly unspoiled street that runs from the beach to Central Avenue. Built mostly at the same time in the mid-1800s, the houses are similar in design, with shingles, gables, porches, and angled rooflines. One of these splendid homes, owned by Fran and Captain Louis Puskas, stands on the corner lot, surrounded by old cedars, beach plum, wild roses, shad bushes, and bayberry.

It seems that 12th Street was one of the earliest developed areas of Barnegat Light. In *The Lure of Long Beach*, published in 1936, author Charles Edgar Nash writes that "in the opinion of Ralph G. Collins, the first house built on the northern end of the island near Barnegat Inlet, was the small dwelling later owned by Caleb Parker, familiarly known as 'Dad' Parker, the 'Barnegat Pirate.'" The author estimates the date of the house as far back as 1800. Bart Slaight from Tuckerton was the builder, and he put up Parker's residence and its neighbor, a larger house that was built to take in boarders. This second house was purchased by Jacob Herring and called the Herring House. Mr. Nash then relates that John M. Brown, a salvage worker, who had four sons, bought the Herring House in 1855, rebuilt it, painted it white, and renamed it the Ashley House. According to a 1935 newspaper article titled "Old Times

On this front porch, with its elegant spindles and fretwork, one can imagine fishermen
in the old days spinning their tall tales of shipwrecks and fishing triumphs.

at Barnegat Inlet," by R. G. Collins (presumably the same gentleman referred to by Mr. Nash), the Ashley House was a "Low long whitewashed structure that had entertained many sportsmen in its day." The Browns ran the Ashley House as a hostelry until 1862, when they sold it. The two subsequent owners went on welcoming local gunners and fishermen until 1882, when the house was abandoned and then torn down.

In these documents there is no reference to a third house on 12th Street—the one on the corner now owned by the Puskas family. It was built by Bart Slaight a few years later than the Parker House or the Ashley House. Its original owner was Benjamin Franklin Archer Sr., who had a quarter share in it with his firm, the Archer Land Company, early developers of Barnegat City. The house took three years to build and was completed in 1859, with lumber brought in by barge. (At that time there were still no roads.) It was large and extravagant, even for the standards of the time. Its exterior is cedar shingle, designed in an adaptation of the Stick style, with a porch with bracketed arches, balconies with spindles on the first and second floors, gabled roofs, high chimneys, and four evenly spaced dormers. According to Captain Puskas, in an early photograph of Barnegat Light, the house appears with a spire on top, like a church. This was replaced at some point with the small widow's walk that now decorates the highest point of the roofline. (Another photograph of 12th Street, taken in 1900, shows that several of the houses on the street had similar turrets and steeples. These were also later removed, owing to their tendency to leak.)

Inside, a sense of grandeur prevails. The ceilings are ten feet high. There are nine bedrooms, three of them with fireplaces, five bathrooms, a huge kitchen, a stairwell made of mahogany, Southern Plantation–style pocket doors dividing the public rooms, and, according to local author Mary Karch, "an entrance hall big enough to put a sailboat in." It is probable that Mr. Archer took in boarders; the house was clearly designed with enough rooms to be rented. (This fact has probably given rise to the confusion in some quarters between the Archer house and the Ashley House.) The Archer house is not sited facing the ocean, as is the custom today, but facing west towards the saltwater lagoon, where, before the arrival of roads and summer houses, the owners could see their sailboat bobbing in the calm waters of Barnegat Bay.

The Archer family continued to dominate the development of Barnegat Inlet. In 1881 they formed the Barnegat City Improvement Company and, thanks to the explosive growth of the town, they became very wealthy. They built two hotels, the Oceanic on East 4th Street and The Sunset on West 5th Street. Neither exists today. In 1885 they also built three more houses on 12th Street, including one for Benjamin Franklin Archer's son George. The house is now called the Archer-Zieber House. Stories about the Archers are still told today, for instance, that eccentric George persuaded his rich father to invest in an ice house business in Honduras. Needless to say, the project failed.

The big corner house on 12th Street was kept in the family until 1975, when it was bought by Fran and Louis Puskas. Lou Puskas is a commercial fishing-boat captain and co-owner of Viking Village dock, and is steeped in the lore of the old Barnegat fishing community. Fishing is still a thriving business and many young locals still take it up as a way of life. "Most of them are natives," Captain Puskas says. "They grew up in the industry, worked on the boats and got a lot of sea time in."

The houses on 12th Street, nestling in their wild and overgrown landscape of old trees, shrubs, and beach plants, still give off the flavor of this old maritime community. Looking at them today, one can easily imagine veteran sea captains sitting on their porches relating fishing stories as the ocean waves dash against the beach at the end of the street, telling their own timeless tales.

Loveladies

"THE HOUSE IS ALMOST LIKE A BRIDGE."

The names of the towns on Long Beach Island are quirky, to say the least. Ship Bottom and Harvey Cedars sound more like the names of cocktails or characters in a Mark Twain novel than shore communities. The name Loveladies is equally provocative, but its origin turns out to be perfectly respectable. The town was developed by Thomas Lovelady, a hunter who spent a lot of time in the area in the late 1890s shooting ducks. Its defining distinction from some of the other Long Beach Island towns is that in 1962 it was flooded in an overwhelming storm that destroyed most of its houses, leaving a wasteland, or rather, in the eyes of architects and developers, a tabula rasa on which they might construct their new and contemporary visions.

The northern and southern ends of Long Beach Island still have some houses and other structures that remind the visitor of its early, wild, and piratical past. As one moves into the center of the island, however, it becomes a New World symphony of pastiche Shingle mansions, cement-block towers, contemporary Cape Cods, thirties ocean liners, and other postmodern fantasies that fulfill the current dreams of summer residents of the Jersey Shore.

Loveladies today has an impressive number of large and very modern houses that run the gamut of styles borrowed from Frank Lloyd Wright, Mies van der Rohe, Philip Johnson, Richard Meier, and Frank Gehry, among others. However, in the midst of these various architectural statements, one local architect has made Loveladies a place very much his own. In March 1989, Michael Ryan moved his firm into an office in Loveladies that had been a 1950s commercial building. He is still there today. Michael Ryan Architects is now a full-service architectural firm; his wife, Randee Spelkoman, is the in-house interior designer, and his staff helps with all aspects of construction and furnishing. Ryan has built several

FACING *The Kaplans collected a series of iron-sculpted birds, all with different expressions, which nestle in the long grasses bordering the driveway to the house.*

There are windows on both sides of the multi-level living-dining area of the house, allowing spectacular views of both the Atlantic and Barnegat Bay. **ABOVE** *A sculptural element is the skylight window overlooking the staircase to the bedrooms on the second floor.*

houses in Loveladies, as well as others in New Jersey and Pennsylvania. But it is quite clear that building on the shore in his hometown is his favorite assignment.

He has said that Loveladies "is like a campground, without a history or identity." Thanks to its long history and geological and physical changes, it is like all barrier islands, he says, which are "placeless places, context-free, neither urban or suburban." This perspective allows enormous freedom to the architect, and Michael Ryan is very well aware of this. In the case of the Kaplan house, he has worked in a vernacular that is modest yet grand, responding to both the requirements of his clients and the demands of the location.

ABOVE *The beachfront side of the house, designed in 1998 by Michael Ryan, shows its impressive length—the size of two or three beachfront lots together—giving the architect room to maneuver while respecting the natural line of the shore.*
FACING *The view of the house from the rear shows its elegant rectangular lines, reflecting those of the pool.*

FACING *The architect placed the swimming pool and pool house at the rear of the house, making linear use of the site without interrupting its open access to the shore.*
ABOVE *The staircase that goes up from the patio to the second-floor living areas flies up into space like an abstract sculpture.*
RIGHT *An eleven-foot open area at ground level offers a vista through to the dunes and ocean. This meant sacrificing a garage, but the owners instead enjoy an uninterrupted view.*

The lower deck's open view towards the ocean is given sculptural drama by the staircase running up to the second floor.

The Kaplans hired Michael Ryan in 1998, after a long search. The family had rented on Long Beach Island for many years, but with their children grown they decided they wanted a more permanent place. They bought a house on the shore in Loveladies in 1997, knowing they would tear it down. They lived in it for a year, "to get the feel of the place and the site," Barbara Kaplan says. Enter Michael Ryan.

The Kaplans and the architect worked closely on every aspect of the design. "When I was wrong he told me," Barbara Kaplan says with a laugh. But in the end, the site spoke for itself, and the architectural decisions were largely based on its unique qualities. It is actually the size of two or three lots together—in other words, unusually large for a shore project. Michael Ryan's first challenge was how to take advantage of that space. "The idea of the pool and pool house at the back of the house made linear use of the site while effectively expanding it," he explains.

Another striking architectural aspect of the house is its openness on both sides. Most beach houses face towards the view, that is, the ocean, leaving the street façade unadorned and protective of privacy. The huge living room windows of the Kaplan house offer vistas both to the Atlantic and to Barnegat Bay. "A further advantage of the house is that the surrounding lots cannot be subdivided," Mr. Ryan points out. "This means the site has a permanently unobstructed view on both sides. Thus the house is almost like a bridge, spanning the ocean and the bay."

An unusual shore bird greets visitors from its nest in the high grasses banking the driveway.

The most original element of the house, however, is its eleven-foot-high open area at ground level that offers a vista through to the dunes and ocean. "The reason for this is that the Kaplans were willing to forgo a garage," the architect says. "That was a real help, so we could use the ground floor as something else than the two-car garage that most summer people insist upon." The architect is grateful to his clients for this concession, which has transformed an otherwise unappealing space into a delightful covered piazza leading to the beach.

In 2003 the Kaplan house won a bronze medal from the New Jersey chapter of the American Institute of Architects, not the first award Ryan's firm has won for its work on both private houses and institutional buildings. But perhaps one of the greatest prizes awarded to Michael Ryan is the lasting friendship that has been created between him and the Kaplans. In an unusual tribute last summer, Michael, his wife, and associate Christopher Jeffrey all attended the wedding of the Kaplans' daughter in Santa Barbara. How often in the history of architect–client relations could that kind of invitation possibly be imagined? 🦐

Spray Beach

"THE AUNT HILL"

Spray Beach is one of the smallest communities on Long Beach Island, and sits at its narrowest point, discreetly tucked away to the north of its much bigger sister, Beach Haven. Originally called Waverly Beach or Cranberry Hill, Spray Beach began its progress into modernity in the late 1880s, when beachfront developers, recognizing the attraction of the recently built Spray Beach Hotel, fingered the land as yet another potential gold mine in terms of vacation real estate. (The hotel was torn down in 1969, and the Spray Beach Inn was built on the site.)

This wonderful little box of a cottage at 205 East 25th Street, known to everyone as "The Aunt Hill," was built between 1887 and 1890 by four sisters named Emma, Rebecca, Mary Anna, and Caroline Newbold, whose family came from Burlington County, New Jersey. Their father, Thomas Jefferson Newbold, was a farmer, and some of the lumber from his house, "Cabin Farm," in Springfield Township, was used to construct his daughters' summer cottage. The wood was brought by wagon and then shipped by barge from Manahawkin across Barnegat Bay to Long Beach Island, which is how most heavy things were brought over to the island before the bridge was built.

The house was originally called "Sea Crest," and its site, designated the Newbold Tract, on 25th Street off Atlantic Avenue, was originally part of a land grant from King George III. Old photographs show the house standing alone on the dunes, like many early shore cottages, before the world moved in and transformed the deserted sandy landscape into desirable vacation homes. Its survival is a wonderful testament to family solidarity lasting for more than a hundred years.

FACING *This miniature gem of a cottage was built between 1887 and 1890 by the four Newbold sisters. It was constructed on part of a land grant from King George III and is quite unique architecturally, with its steeply pitched roof, gable, and box-like floor plan. Its secret is its breathtaking simplicity, along with the fact that it has outlasted almost every McMansion the summer getaway crowd has cared to throw up around it.*

Farmer Newbold had seven daughters in all, but only one married. She was Sarah Shreve Newbold, and she married James Woolman Deacon. Their granddaughter, Sarah Newbold Deacon, married Richard Doane Bates. The house in Spray Beach entered the Bates family when the four Newbold aunts bequeathed it in the 1930s to Sarah Bates, their only grand-niece. The Bateses kept it until after World War II, when it was acquired by a Philadelphian named Mary Martin Wharton Miller. When she died, she left the house to the ASPCA, who put it up for sale. Sarah Bates heard it was on the market and repurchased it in 1961.

Ross and Jane Gilfillan, who owned rental property on the other side of Atlantic Avenue, had admired it greatly over the years, and finally were able to buy it from the Bates family in 2003. Ever since, with the help of their four children, they have been lovingly restoring it to its former simple glory.

Its modest beauty embraces a shopping list of architectural treats. It has a steeply pitched roof, with a gable and an open porch facing south, east, and west, with exposed rafter tails in the floor joists. The exterior shingles are made of New Jersey white cedar. The house has never been painted in all its days, so these cedar shakes are absolutely pristine, although it is possible that the exterior was originally clapboard. Inside, there is a lot of mahogany trim, which, according to the present owner and historian of the house, Jane Gilfillan, was used

frequently as ballast on ships. "The ships would offload the wood and local residents would quickly retrieve it to build their houses."

The house originally had shutters, and the porch was probably added later, according to Richard E. Plunkett, chairman of Historic Homes of Long Beach Island and owner of the quirky antiques shop, The Wizard of Odds, in Beach Haven Crest. "This is one of my favorite houses on the island," he declares. "It's so basic and simple, what I would call 'Quaker Victorian.' " Mr. Plunkett points to another unique aspect of Aunt Hill—it is built on sand, unlike the gravel or concrete that formed the foundation of most other houses of the period.

One final piece of history—its change of name. "The house is blessed to be over twelve feet above sea level," Jane points out, "which may have contributed to the 'hill' part of the name, and has also helped it weather the many storms buffeting it throughout its 115-year history." It remained standing—with damage only to the southeast corner of the porch—even after the famous storm of 1962, which destroyed many houses on the island. This history of resilience is all the more impressive considering the cottage's sand foundations.

As for the "aunt" part of its name, the amusing wordplay is easy to explain once you know its history. "It was called The Aunt Hill because my four great-grandaunts lived there at the turn of the century," explains Sarah Bates's son, Richard.

From "The Aunt Hill," which was built on sand, not the usual concrete, it is a straight shot to the dunes and beach.

Beach Haven

ALMOST PERFECT SUMMER RESORT ARCHITECTURE

Towards the southernmost tip of Long Beach Island lies Beach Haven. It is sometimes fondly described as lying "six miles at sea." This means it is separated from the mainland by five miles or more of the open waters of Little Egg Harbor Bay. Originally, like much of the Jersey Shore, it was a mostly uninhabited spot, home to wild birds, fish, the Lenni Lenape Indians, and a few dedicated hunters. Archelaus R. Pharo of Tuckerton is credited with envisioning the area as a potential summer resort in 1873; his daughter named it Beach Haven. In 1874 Pharo and his friend Dr. Alfred Smith of Philadelphia built the first cottages there on Second Street. Both still stand, now numbered 121 and 125. (Pharo's house is called Louella Cottage.) At the same time, the Tuckerton and Long Beach Building, Land and Improvement Association began serious development of the town; the Quakers moved in from Philadelphia and built a meeting house; and in 1875, giving the ultimate imprimatur of a summer destination to Beach Haven, the Engleside Hotel opened for visitors. All self-respecting resorts must have a yacht club, and the Beach Haven Yacht Club was formed in 1876. The Ocean House and Magnolia House both opened in 1877.

In the familiar story of the development of the New Jersey coastline, the apotheosis of Beach Haven occurred in May 1886, when the Pennsylvania Railroad began service from Philadelphia to Beach Haven. The still modest town was immediately transformed into a major summer place. In an unpublished history compiled by retired postmaster Harry L. Willits, he reports that records show there were at least ten trains a day during the summer months. According to a 1914 history of Long Beach Island by George B. Somerville, an interesting extra selling point offered by the town was that "The Weather Bureau reports show the temperature at Beach Haven to range from five to ten degrees cooler throughout the summer months than at other New Jersey resorts not located on Long Beach."

FACING *Unique to the Jersey Shore, indeed perhaps anywhere in the world, is this delightful architectural flourish— a stencil-like incised vase of flowers, one of a pair inserted between the second-floor windows of the cottage.*

137

House-building boomed. Large cottages, built in the expansive Victorian manner of the period, lined the main streets of Beach Avenue, Engleside Avenue, and Bay Avenue, many of them owned by senior railroad executives. One of the most attractive rows of cottages formed the nucleus of Coral Street, which runs from the ocean to Bay Avenue (now Long Beach Boulevard). The reason for their charm is that several of them were built by the same architectural firm, giving them a unity of style that is not always found in the resort towns that exploded so dramatically at the beginning of the twentieth century. The firm was called Wilson Brothers and Co., based in Philadelphia. Both brothers, John A. Wilson and Joseph M. Wilson, started their careers as engineers with the Pennsylvania Railroad, John specializing in the building of railways, his brother an expert in bridges and institutional buildings. Their chief architect was Frederick Thorn, who seems to have had no academic architectural training, but had a practice in North Carolina until the Civil War, when he was involved in the construction of military hospitals.

The firm built many well-known buildings, including the Philadelphia Subway, the Philadelphia and Reading Railroad Terminal, and the Broad Street Station of the Pennsylvania Railroad. But by the mid-1880s, the Wilson Brothers had acquired several important private residential commissions in New York, New Jersey, and Pennsylvania, many of them on the Jersey Shore, tapping into the newly desirable land opened up as the Pennsylvania Railroad moved down the coast. "Seaside cottages" in Atlantic City and Spring Lake are listed in their 1885 catalog of commissions, but the biggest number are located in Beach Haven. In 1882 they built the town's first Episcopal church, Holy Innocents' Mission Church, a glorious fantasy in wood and Gothic detailing that is now the Long Beach Island Historical Museum.

Perhaps inspired by this architectural delight, the Wilsons then turned to Coral Street, where John and his firm created at least three small masterpieces, including 123 Coral Street. This two-and-a-half-story, five-bay house was built in 1882 for Dr. E. H. Williams, but for unrecorded reasons he did not keep it, selling it back to the architect a year later in 1883. The Wilson family lived in it for a hundred years before selling it in 1983 to the present owners, a consortium of nine friends.

TOP *Yet another sad and threatening sight along the shore—but in this case, restorers have come to the rescue.* **ABOVE** *A note of gratitude for the saviors of this fine old shore house.*

This Beach Haven masterpiece is the perfect expression of late–nineteenth-century summer resort architecture,
with its hipped and diamond-tile roofs, gabled dormers, Tudor-style half-timbering, and spectacular brick chimneys.

The spindle balustrades on the first and second floors, the floor-to-ceiling ground-floor windows, plus the delicate stencil-style flower decoration, give the façade of this house an extraordinary elegance.

One can quite understand why the Wilson family kept it so long. The house is an almost perfect expression of summer resort architecture produced at the end of the nineteenth century. It has Victorian-style uneven hipped roofs, gabled dormers on the east and west façades, an open porch protected by a first-floor roof, and two extraordinary brick chimneys linked by an arch. The ground-floor windows are floor-to-ceiling, measuring nine feet high, an unusual Italianate feature. The porch runs along all four sides of the house, with elegant turned balustrades and spindles. The second floor has a recessed balcony with a similar balustrade.

Perhaps the most delightful feature is the stencil-like incised pattern of flowers at the center of each gable between the pairs of second-floor windows, a unique decorative flourish.

The Wilson Brothers' 1885 catalog lists the construction of four private residences in Beach Haven, including two designed for Charles and William Parry at 127 and 135 Coral Street, and 111 Coral Street, designed for George Burnham. The fourth, owned by John Wilson, is 123 Coral Street and is illustrated in the catalog. The picture shows that the original gables of 123 were half-timbered, and the windows had shutters. Although this illustration is in black and white, current co-owner David Cronrath says that the original colors were light lime green with dark green trim and India-red sash.

There is also an indication in the Wilson drawing of other houses behind 123 Coral Street on what is now Amber Street. Mrs. Wilson had them built for her three unmarried daughters. Someone in the family must have been an enthusiast of William Shakespeare, for each of these cottages on Amber Street was named for a character from one of the Bard's plays: Rosalind is number 18, Silvia number 122, and Audrey number 126. Portia Cottage is the name for 123 Coral Street. All four houses in this mini-compound have been wittily referred to as Shakespeare's "Hamlet." (Naming houses was nothing new during this period of Beach Haven's development: 127 Coral Street is called "Florence Cottage," not in honor of Shakespeare, but in honor of Charles Parry's granddaughter, Florence Brunner.)

As already noted, the houses on Coral Street have an unusual architectural felicity in their similarity of style. This seems to have caused a little trouble from time to time. There is a story that the son of one of the Coral Street residents liked to indulge somewhat during his summer vacations, and on coming back late at night would get the houses confused and show up on the doorstep of the wrong one. This slight inconvenience to the neighbors was remedied by the erection of a flag in the garden so the inebriated scion of the family might find his way home.

Today, this no longer seems to be a problem; instead, several of the houses are threatened by demolition. The nine owners of 123 Coral Street, however, have carefully tended to their historic property, replacing roof tiles and repainting, but otherwise retaining its original appearance. And now, after more than twenty years of ownership, the nine friends' children and grandchildren come and enjoy the summers here, a gift to this lovely old house that it must surely appreciate.

Brigantine

"WE DECIDED TO PAINT THE BANDS
A GOOD STRONG COLOR."

Brigantine is said to have been named after a shipwreck in the eighteenth century. At that time it was an unprotected spit of land surrounded by the marshes and bays of Absecon, and was famous for its fierce winds and dangerous currents.

Brigantine was a late bloomer. In 1878, for instance, it was described in the Woolman & Rose *Atlas* as a "low, sandy, barren island. Two hotels for summer boarders are found here, Holdzkom's and Smith's, and a number of private residences have been erected on its southern part since the popular growth of Atlantic City." T. E. Rose, the author of this work, was very perceptive. He described the situation perfectly. Even then, Brigantine was seen as a satellite of the vibrant, noisy city immediately to its south. It still is.

The earliest, primitive phase of Brigantine soon developed into a typical bedroom community, mostly spill-over during the 1970s from the invasion of casino workers from Atlantic City. Today, however, as with so many shore destinations, that modest description is under review. If one drives around Brigantine, one still sees the bungalows and little two-story cottages that belong to people who work in Atlantic City, but as the new century progresses, they are gradually being squeezed out or torn down and replaced by the huge mansions that are rising up in giant waves of construction around them. With pretty water views on both sides of the island, and with the addition in Atlantic City of yet another huge casino, the Borgata, Brigantine is on the way to becoming another upscale dream resort.

But there are elements of Brigantine that keep it real. Unlike many of the shore resorts exploding with wealthy investment and uncontrolled development, Brigantine sits in the permanently looming shadow of the skyline of Atlantic City. At twilight, the huge dark casino blocks point heavenward like a reminder to all those within their shade of our all-too-human frailty. There is also a more practical aspect to Brigantine's sense of proportion. Providing

FACING *The owners of this striking house took on the architecture and design of it themselves. Their imagination, fueled by exposure to other new houses going up along the shore, produced a fascinating amalgam of Art Deco, Cubist, and Palladian styles, all pulled together by the teal-colored bands wrapped around the white stucco façade.*

ABOVE AND FACING *Atlantic City, far from the crowds, the casinos, the neon and the sound of money, reveals another side, its cement pillars, like ancient colonnades, caught in a moment of desolation and timeless beauty.*

The sinuous exterior spiral stair winding up to the roof, combined with the blocks of glass and stucco, give the rear of the house the feel of a 1920s abstract sculpture.

a further disincentive to excess, the lots available on Brigantine are quite small, affording an interesting challenge to those who wish to build a serious summer house.

Daniel and Eugenia Ciechanowski faced this challenge when acquiring their lot on the inland waterway of Brigantine thirteen years ago. Dr. Ciechanowski's parents had a summer house in Brigantine, and he remembered happy summers there. After moving off the island to pursue his career as a dentist, he finally settled in an office in nearby Galloway and began looking with his wife for a permanent place back on the island of his childhood. After settling on this appealing piece of land, they proceeded to design and build the house themselves. Astonishingly, the whole process took hardly more than a year.

The biggest issue was how best to exploit the relatively small footprint of the lot without making the house look like a cube. "My wife made the sketches, and we brought in an architect to make measured drawings," says Dr. Ciechanowski. "The rest of the work we did ourselves."

They got some of their ideas from driving around parts of the shore where new houses were going up, such as Margate and Longport. "We liked the architecture of the late Robert Johnson," Dr. Ciechanowski observes, "in particular the synthetic stucco that he liked to use." They used the same stucco on their own house. It worked well with the architectural details they chose, which are largely Art Deco in style, with crenellations, curved glass windows, columns, and a spiral staircase at the back of the house reaching up to an observation platform on the roof. A high stoop facing the street elevates the front entrance of the house above ground level, eliminating any possibility of a boxy feel.

One of the most striking elements of the house is the series of horizontal painted "bands" on the façade. The owners call the rich aquamarine color "teal," and it highlights the interesting, almost Cubist lines of the house. "Originally it was all white," Dr. Ciechanowski says, "but the effect was a little flat, so we decided to paint the bands a good strong color."

When space is at a premium, designers must come up with ingenious methods of disguising the limitations of a small parcel of land. The Ciechanowskis found a way of making the most of a beautiful setting, while building a house that is both bold and economical in design, a fine solution for their new life in Brigantine.

Family-friendly, the house has a flight of stoop-like steps leading to the front door, so that the interior is elevated, opening it up to light and views.

"WE WANTED EVERY ROOM TO HAVE A VIEW."

One of the most intriguing sights for visitors crossing the bridge from Atlantic City to Brigantine is a large, dramatically sited house that faces the inland waterway. Clean of line, simple of structure, and noticeably pink, it catches the eye as the sun slowly goes down after a long summer's day on the island.

The house belongs to Richard and Mary Caruso. It was begun in 1988 and completed in 1991. The Carusos designed it themselves, with a mixture of originality and verve that makes it quite unique as a shore home.

Richard Caruso was a hair stylist for forty years, and during this time he invented a form of hair rollers that became enormously successful. The Carusos spent many years traveling to promote this product, also wishing to visit out-of-the-way places that would inspire them when they got home. Richard Caruso was always artistic, and travel satisfied his creative spirit.

They purchased the land in Brigantine in 1988, and Richard immediately hired a pair of architects to draw up some plans. As is often the case in Brigantine, the lot was difficult, angular and oddly sited, and the architects, after three attempts, failed to come up with anything that pleased their clients. At this point, says Mary Caruso, Richard took over. "He drew up his own plans, mapping out the footprint, finding out about codes, and finally making a scale model." The couple then found an architect to make the professional drawings required, and the house got built.

The architecture reflects the interests of the owners. During his travels, Richard would always make sketches of houses and buildings. "He was always interested in architecture, and perhaps in another life he would have been an architect," Mary says. They went to Europe, Asia, Hawaii, and Egypt. "I remember when the Tutankhamen exhibition opened at the British Museum in London," she recalls, "there was a very long line, and we were practically the last people to go in, but it impressed us both immensely and we never forgot it."

The influences of Egypt are apparent in the façade of the house, as are the influences of modern art and architecture. (Richard Meier comes to mind.) "We also wanted every room to have a view," she points out. "That meant the house had to be open everywhere to the outside." The result is a striking mixture of modernism and antiquity. Even the garden that

FACING *The enormous pink mansion that towers over the inland waterway in Brigantine is one of the most dramatic sights of the Jersey Shore. Its color, length, and structural complexity are like a constant challenge to the summer sun, which profligately casts its light and shadows over the house like a long-running movie.*

ABOVE *The house is a mixture of styles: the Egyptian motif over the garage is one; the huge California-style windows are another; and the soft pink color of the façade was inspired by trips to the Caribbean and Hawaii.* **FACING TOP** *The formalistic two-story flying buttresses that create a massive exterior loggia and give the house its stylistic anchor are reminiscent of the architecture of Richard Meier's Getty Center in Los Angeles, California.* **FACING BOTTOM** *Under the loggia, one may sit and reflect on the temptations offered by the casinos of Atlantic City beckoning in the distance.*

ABOVE *The garden in front of the house, designed
and planted by Richard Caruso, is a charming oasis
of soothing greenery, largely influenced by gardens
the Carusos have visited in California and Japan.*
RIGHT *The aluminum railings that
encircle the deck are like those on an
ocean liner, with the water directly below.*

stretches out in front of the house—which Richard Caruso planted himself—has the feel of both Japan and California.

The color of the house is perhaps its most interesting feature. It was Mary Caruso's idea. "We have been to all the Caribbean islands," she explains, "as well as Hawaii and Bermuda. I had always noticed in those places that pink is a soft shade in the sun. And this house gets a lot of sun."

The rear side of the house was the first to receive the paint. When her husband saw it as he was driving across the bridge, he stopped the car, parked it, turned to his wife, and said, "I hate it!"

It was Friday afternoon. Mary Caruso thought of the fifty-five gallons of paint waiting to be applied, and took a deep breath. She called the painter and he said he would repaint the whole house white, and that he would begin on Monday. Meanwhile, Richard sat in the sand on a rocker all weekend (the deck was not yet built), and on Monday morning he turned to Mary and said, "I love it!" So the color stayed, and as the sun moves around the house, the color changes at different times of the day, just as she had envisaged.

Today it's a year-round vacation place, often filled with children and grandchildren. Its spectacular views and striking elevations make it a fascinating living space. The Carusos love to reminisce about their exciting travels, and their house in Brigantine is a monument to remind them of all the places they have been.

In spite of its imposing architecture, the house provides several private places for a peaceful time-out from the many family members who visit on vacations.

Stone Harbor

" WE WANTED TO CREATE A MODERN
HOUSE IN AN OLD STYLE. *"*

In all the debates and discussions about historic preservation and the restoration of old houses, nothing is more controversial than the matter of past versus present, old architecture versus new architecture, old materials versus new materials, original versus copy. In England, where the tradition of living in old houses is as irreversible as the country's history, the crisis of modern architecture hinges to some extent on the question of whether to maintain the beauty of the Tudor, Elizabethan, Queen Anne, or Georgian styles so beloved of the British, or whether to abandon all these old styles entirely and build new glass boxes. Prince Charles famously called one such proposal "a monstrous carbuncle" on the landscape—an example of the emotions the whole subject provokes.

In the United States, these issues are less frenzied since there is a comparably small inventory of historic architecture to fight over. In England, the National Trust is an enormous, powerful organization that can raise hundreds of thousands of pounds in a few months to save a threatened house (as happened in the case of Tyntesfield, a Victorian mansion near Bristol), but in the United States the National Trust is a small, struggling body of enthusiasts who have neither the money nor the clout to rescue many of the country's older buildings. While preservation architects spend much of their valuable time fighting local and state authorities over the future of a historically important house, many people do not understand the point of wasting tears over a pile of old, crumbling bricks or wood when a glamorous, state-of-the-art, streamlined contemporary-style residence can be built instead.

The Jersey Shore is a classic battleground for these opposing values. Much of its early history can be seen in the splendid cottages that still dot the coastal landscape from Atlantic Highlands to Cape May. Most of these were built at the turn of the nineteenth century,

FACING *The hidden waterways of Grassy Sound, near Stone Harbor, are reluctant to reveal their secrets.*

when the region was beginning to be discovered and appreciated. Over the years, this appreciation has transformed the shore from a series of communities—some religious, some wealthy urbanites, some young hedonists—into a highly desirable playground ripe for a developer's greedy tentacles. As the twenty-first century rolls on, the older houses are being torn down and replaced with far more user-friendly holiday homes, and with them real estate is soaring to levels unimaginable to the modest Methodists who put up their tents by the Atlantic a century earlier.

Stone Harbor is an interesting case in this context. It was originally called "Seven Mile Beach," an island off the southern coast of New Jersey, which Aaron Leaming, a resident of Sag Harbor, Long Island, bought in 1722. It was described in the deed as "being an entire island from three quarters of flood to one quarter of ebb, bounded as followeth: On the South east by the main ocean or sea; on the South west by Hereford Inlet and on the Northeast by the inlet called Townsends Inlet." During these early years, Mr. Leaming evidently did not make much of his distant property; it was used as pastureland by mainland farmers who managed to persuade their cattle to swim across the channel in the spring and back to the mainland before the frost. (The county courthouse holds a record of the identifying marks the farmers branded on their cows' ears.)

By the beginning of the twentieth century, however, swimming cows had been replaced by the railroad and its attendant real estate speculators. The first hotel, the Abbotsford Inn, was erected in 1892, and cottages began to sprout up alongside it. Stone Harbor's major developer was the South Jersey Realty Company, which bought up much of the territory of

ABOVE *The bridge to Stone Harbor and the Wildwoods carries thousands of holidaymakers to the shore every summer while a tiny community, mostly unknown and unrecognized, lives in its shadow.*
RIGHT *Simply constructed wooden cottages are connected by rickety boardwalks that stretch endlessly across the lonely marshes towards the horizon.*

Stone Harbor in 1907 and promptly started marketing it to interested buyers. Describing its beauties and charms ("The Long Island of Philadelphia!" "The Wonder City by the Sea!"), the company assuaged prospective buyers' anxiety about its inaccessibility by promising the construction of a causeway that would link Stone Harbor to Cape May Court House. "Seashore property has passed entirely out of the field of speculation," declared the brochure, "and has become a solid, substantial investment."

This confident—indeed, visionary—proposal was the brainchild of the Risley family, who owned the company and was responsible for the development of Stone Harbor into its present-day form. The town's only drawback was inaccessibility, but when Governor Woodrow Wilson opened the Stone Harbor Ocean Parkway on Monday, July 3, 1911, its fate was secured. The usual succession of houses, sailing clubs, churches, and schools was built as the community expanded. Unlike the houses built on the northern shore, Stone Harbor architecture seems to be more straightforwardly Victorian, with a four-square boxy floor plan, gables, steep roofs, and two-story balustraded balconies.

Today, one's first impression is that little has changed. Unlike many other Jersey resorts, Stone Harbor has retained its quiet elegance over the years, without the fast-food or

*The traditional clapboard façade, portico, and gingerbread and dentil decoration
are painted in soft shades of gray, blending into the fabric of the community.*

This house is only nine years old, but its careful attention to historic shore architecture, including wraparound porches on two stories, a tower with a turret, uneven rooflines, balustrades, and spindles, gives it the quiet elegance of the Victorian cottages it has replaced.

motel-style junkiness that has infected so many of these ocean communities. Street after street of large, Victorian-style cottages seem to give the town the feeling of a time warp. Look more closely, however, and you will see that a considerable number of these clapboard, balconied mansions are not old at all. In fact, they are quite new.

Bona Scarpa's house, for instance, is only nine years old.

Ms. Scarpa discovered the quiet lure of Stone Harbor just over nine years ago. One block from the beach, on a corner plot, the original house had gone, succumbing to the fate of time and obsolescence. In its place were the foundations of a new building. "It was a wonderful site," Ms. Scarpa recalls. "I wanted it at once."

But then Ms. Scarpa had to confront another decision—in the place of a former Victorian gem, what to build instead? Since the house was not yet constructed, she could write her own ticket, so to speak. In consultation with Donald Zacker of the the Zacker Group, based in Avalon, who was the architect in charge of the site, Bona Scarpa studied the history, looked at pictures, and settled on a design that would both recognize the past and yet satisfy the needs of a modern house-owner. "We wanted to keep the Victorian flavor," she says. "My daughter is an architect and understands the historical nature of the town's architecture. We wanted to create a modern house in an old style."

They achieved this by accepting the major Victorian conventions—a clapboard façade; wraparound porches on both first- and second-floor levels; a tower with a turret; uneven rooflines; and balustrades and spindles. The two-tone grays with red detailing reflect the original color palette of Stone Harbor's nineteenth- and early-twentieth-century cottages. The architects also incorporated Victorian-style gingerbread and dentil work that ornament the exterior of the house. In another salute to traditional architecture, the house is "upside-down" in design—that is, the living and kitchen areas are upstairs on the second floor, where one can see the view of the ocean, a very common floor plan for early shore homes.

"We wanted to fit in with the environment, and not lose the history of the neighborhood," says Ms. Scarpa. Her architect agrees. "We design a house like this to blend into the fabric of the community," Donald Zacker explains, "reminiscent of the old shapes and forms of the historical architecture."

Their effort to blend old and new has its difficulties. For instance, the spindles—slender, turned columns that support the porch—are difficult to make, and few carpenters have the skill to reproduce them. But Ms. Scarpa's dilemma of building on a vacant lot where historic architecture once stood has been solved to everyone's satisfaction. The carefully thought-out design of her nine-year-old house brings back happy memories of the one-hundred-year-old house that she replaced, its vanished presence like a friendly ghost welcoming the new heirs of a long-lived tradition. 🦑

"A MOST ATTRACTIVE DWELLING."

In one of the earliest photographs of Stone Harbor, taken from the Pennsylvania Railroad Plaza, a strange new house sits alone in front of a group of four or five "cottages" being constructed after the railroad arrived in 1892. Unlike the other cottages, which are made of wood, with the familiar two or three stories, attic dormers, steep roofs, turrets, gables, balconies, and balustrades, this house has only one story (with basement), an apparently flat roof, square columns at the front entrance, and, most oddly, it is built entirely of concrete. It is still unfinished, and it stands out from the empty, flat, undeveloped landscape like an eerie vision from urban New York. Or is it an Egyptian temple rising up out of the sand?

A photograph of the house, taken sometime after 1909, documents its eccentric appearance in relation to the large traditional Victorians going up around it in the early days of Stone Harbor.

This is perhaps the most unusual house on the Jersey Shore. It looks rather like a bank, with its square columns, temple-like portico, concave cornices, and steep flight of steps to the first—and only—floor (above a basement). Gilbert Smith built it around 1909, but how he came to decide on this architectural anomaly is not explained.

ABOVE *Perhaps the most surprising aspect of the house is its construction material—concrete. Its austerity is softened by decorative moldings and balustrades.*
RIGHT *The stern white concrete, so different from the customary clapboard or shingle, is softened by other more familiar shore elements—wooden screen doors and an old wicker armchair.*

The known facts about this astonishing house are as follows: The land was owned (as was most of Stone Harbor) by the South Jersey Realty Company, who sold it to the Gilbert Smith Company of Philadelphia in 1909. On this 5,720-square-foot corner portion of a larger parcel, Gilbert Smith built the house that we see today. It is constructed entirely out of reinforced concrete, still a relatively new building material at that time, used mainly for road and bridge construction, and wildly unusual for private residences. It has only one story, a flat roof, Cavetto (concave) cornices, square pillars and pilasters, geometric door and window moldings, a massive flight of steps ascending to the front door, and a rusticated basement. All these architectural devices are described as Egyptian Revival. The long windows with fanlights flanking the front door and the first-floor balustrades also offer classical references. The concrete roof, though appearing flat, is actually a dome with a central chimney.

Egypt in Stone Harbor? What was Gilbert Smith thinking?

The owner of this singular palace is Joseph Moran, who runs a manufacturing business in Pennsylvania. While looking for a second home in Stone Harbor, he fell in love with this idiosyncratic offering on what is now 86th Street and Pennsylvania Avenue. "It was the only one I looked at." Since then, he has studied the history of his house with the passion of an archaeologist. The questions keep coming. "Why did he use concrete?" Joe asks. "Was he experimenting with it, to see if it would work as a residential material? Was he trying to make the house hurricane-proof? Why select the Egyptian style of architecture? Was it planned as a bank, not a private home? Was the builder wanting to showcase cement as a building material?" Joe concedes that he will probably never know for certain. There is no question, however, that building a concrete house on the sand, which meant digging poured concrete foundations of unusual depth to carry such weight, was a risky and, in the end, triumphant piece of engineering.

Gilbert Smith owned the house until 1927, when it was sold to the Diller family, who ran a store and a realty-development company in Stone Harbor. It appears, however, that Smith never completed the building or lived in it, and that the Dillers bought it unfinished. In 1929, when the Dillers finally moved in, a newspaper advertisement by C. Diller explains that the house "was to have been used by its original builders as a sample home and office." This plan evidently never came to fruition. Mr. Diller goes on to announce that "The White House, on the Plaza, 85th Street and 2nd Avenue, for many years known as the OLD CONCRETE HOUSE . . . WAS COMPLETED THIS MONTH, JULY 1929, by its Present Owners, AND IS NOW OPEN FOR THE INSPECTION of all who wish to see something entirely different in HOME CONSTRUCTION."

It is not known how many people rushed to visit the newly named White House (by which it has been identified ever since), but the Dillers were a major development influence in Stone Harbor then and for many decades to come, and no doubt interest was aroused in this venture, which was very different from the Cape Cod–style houses the Dillers built and sold during the expansion of the town.

The architecture of the house has been called Egyptian Revival. The Egyptian motif is definitively expressed in the window and door moldings.

A newspaper announcement of an estate sale held for Mr. Diller's widow at a later date describes the house as "a poured concrete bank building, which after having stood uncompleted for a number of years, was finally purchased by the Dillers and remodeled into a most attractive dwelling." (That it was described as a bank building suggests that Gilbert Smith may indeed have planned to turn it into a bank.) The bidding on the property reached sixteen thousand dollars when it was withdrawn from the sale, as were the other Diller properties up for auction that day. It was reported that "Mrs. Diller expressed her preference to building on the remaining lots rather than selling below value." (In the end, Mrs. Diller, in an act of community largesse, donated the house to the Borough of Stone Harbor.)

Another odd relic of this period is an advertisement for a one-dollar reward "for every photograph of the old Diller Concrete House now known as The White House, 85th Street and 2nd Avenue, Stone Harbor, BEFORE IT WAS REMODELED." The photographs were to be brought or mailed to Diller's Store, "care of the Portland Cement Association." That last instruction is indicative. Why was the Portland Cement Association so interested, unless it wished to use the house for marketing purposes? Was Diller also in the cement business?

After the Diller sale, the White House had six owners before Joe Moran bought it in 1993. Over the years, very little had been done to the house. A porch was added on the south side, and a small larder off the kitchen at the back. Its concrete construction has stood the test of time, and it still looks much as it looked when it was completed in 1909.

What is different is the context of the house, its surroundings. Instead of standing alone like a desert monument in glorious isolation as it did in 1909, with a nearby assortment of modest cottages like the Cape Cods built by the Dillers, it is now surrounded by enormous new mansions that in recent years have begun replacing those simpler buildings. Instead of the White House towering over its neighbors, now it is overshadowed by these multi-story, multi-decked extravaganzas.

But the White House still stops traffic.

It is clear that the other early purchasers of Stone Harbor property were less than overwhelmed by Gilbert Smith's eccentric investment. As far as is known, no other reinforced concrete Egyptian Revival house exists in Stone Harbor, or indeed anywhere else on the Jersey Shore. Snowbirds were perhaps not interested in building a house that looked more like the Merchants Exchange in Philadelphia than a summer cottage. Now, of course, it arouses intense interest from visitors passing by. How fortunate that nobody wished to erase this unique architectural experiment from the stylish streetscape of Stone Harbor. The White House remains a delightful anomaly.

Cape May Point

"I SPENT YEARS RESEARCHING THE COLORS, CHANGING THEM UNTIL I WAS HAPPY WITH THEM."

Cape May is probably the most famous resort in New Jersey. Indeed, it is almost equally famous outside New Jersey. People come from all over the world, not only to see its beaches, which are long and white, or to enjoy its restaurants, which are many and varied, but to experience one of the most complete examples of an American Victorian town left in the country. By Victorian we mean authentic Victorian—not a reconstructed, modern interpretation of a Victorian town, not a theme park decorated with Victorian-style houses, not a laborious copy of Victorian architecture. Most of Cape May's gable-and-gingerbread cottages were built during the mid nineteenth to the early twentieth century, as the community grew, and they have stood up to the vagaries of hurricanes, floods, natural deterioration, tourism, and real estate development with the toughness of an old sea captain holding his mainsail to the wind.

However, while visitors flock into Cape May, riding on the trolley, admiring the colorful façades, learning the history of these beautiful old places, there is another town, even farther down the shore, right at the western tip of the state, where a few Cape May–style houses have quietly demonstrated their own staying power. Like their neighbor to the north, over one hundred years they have had the benefit—and good luck—of having owners who understood their quality and rarity, and who managed to resist change. The place is Cape May Point.

FACING *The last outpost of the Jersey Shore returns to nature at Cape May Point.*

*The home of an old sea captain
is emblematic of the long history
and culture of this great old town
at the southern tip of the state.*

Many people think of Cape May Point as a center for birders. Indeed, it is a haven for migrating birds, and wildlife enthusiasts flock to the area in the spring and fall to see the birds and butterflies who transform this seaside reserve into a magical kingdom.

But it is also a reserve for Victorian cottages. While the spotlight remains firmly fixed on its bigger, more glamorous sister, the quiet, little-populated pathways of Cape May Point are just as likely to boast a gorgeous gingerbread fantasy as downtown Cape May. The visitor who ventures down Yale Avenue will inevitably stumble upon one such house, a house so fascinating that one might think it had been transported in one piece from Cape May itself.

Rosemere Cottage was built in 1875–1876 as a summer home for the Reverend Adolph Spaeth of Philadelphia. The land belonged to the Sea Grove Island Association, which was formed in 1875 to develop the area. The cottage was originally called "Roseneath Cottage," in honor of the Duke of Argyle's family seat in Scotland, where Spaeth lived as a tutor when he was a young man. Adolph Spaeth was born in 1839 in Württemberg, Germany. He was ordained as a minister in the Lutheran Church in 1861, and came to the United States two years later, embarking on a distinguished career as scholar and author. In 1867 he became pastor of St. John's German Lutheran Congregation in Philadelphia, and in 1873 became a professor at Philadelphia's Lutheran Theological Seminary. Author of many books and translations (including Luther's works), in 1880 he married Philadelphian Harriet Reynolds Krauth, daughter of hymn translator Charles Krauth. It is not clear how he found his way to Cape May Point, but he made it his summer home before he was married and then kept it on as a family house until his death (he built a neighboring cottage for his son). His widow lived in Rosemere Cottage until she died in 1925. After a series of owners (and changes), in 1999 Rosemere Cottage came into the hands of Marcina and William Wagner, who own it today.

The house is modest, as befits the young Lutheran minister who commissioned it, but the exuberant Carpenter Gothic architecture is little short of blasphemous. The Reverend Spaeth clearly wanted to inject a little playfulness into his summers on the shore, perhaps as a contrast to the austerity of his pastoral duties in Philadelphia. Rosemere Cottage's builder was Joseph S. Russell, who built several houses in the town. (When Bill Wagner began his restoration work on the house, he discovered a pencil signature on a piece of wood attached to a window on the first floor of the house, which said, "Jos. S. Russell, Cape May City, NJ.") The structure is balloon framed, a common building form at the time, probably originating in the American South around 1804. It consists of small boards nailed together, rather than large post-and-beam timbers, and vertical studs rising from the foundation to the attic without any horizontal breaks. (The word "balloon" comes from the empty cavity between the exterior and interior walls where insulation would be installed.) While popular and easy (balloon-framed houses settled better than platform structures), this form of construction was also a firetrap (the air flowed up through the house without any firebreak), a particularly serious threat to the mostly wooden houses built along the shore in the

*St. Peter's-by-the-Sea in Cape May Point opened its doors in 1880, and its wonderful
Carpenter Gothic or Stick-style architecture has given pleasure to visitors ever since.*

ABOVE *Built in 1875–1876, Rosemere Cottage is one of the shore's finest examples of Carpenter Gothic architecture. Meticulously restored by its owners, its fanciful, colorful gingerbread decoration takes one's breath away.* FACING TOP *The decorative fretwork eaves of the roof cast a lovely shadow down towards the Gothic-style window, with its peaked pediment and shutters.* FACING BOTTOM *The mix of colors tried and tested by Bill Wagner highlights the extraordinary variety of carpentry detailing on the walls, doors, and windows of the cottage.*

nineteenth century. Both for this reason and because the extra-long wall studs became expensive and scarce, balloon-framing went out of fashion in the twentieth century, being used only rarely today.

Rosemere Cottage is full of other original elements—door frames, moldings, chimneys, and garden plantings. Upstairs, there were originally five bedrooms and one bathroom. The cedar trees to the left of the house were mentioned in Spaeth's memoirs, as well as the pebble-and-shell path underneath the lawn that can still be seen from the second-floor deck.

When the Wagners first bought the house it was painted a putty color. The roof was problematic, the porch was screened, and the garden untended. But the gingerbread decoration was all in place, all original, each piece different. Bill Wagner quickly went to work on his Carpenter Gothic masterpiece. He replaced the original cedar-shake roofs with patterned asphalt and fiberglass shingles. He installed proper heating (he and his wife live in the house

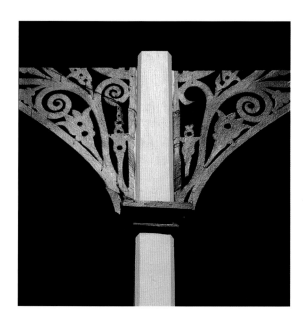

year-round). He replaced some windows. Inside Rosemere Cottage, the rooms are small, but interestingly designed in the Arts and Crafts manner, with wide random-width beam floors, stained pine screens dividing the public rooms, and pine moldings. The Wagners respected this period flavor, adding their own Arts and Crafts pieces to the decorative mix.

But the revival of the gingerbread carpentry work was the Wagners' most important and rewarding challenge. "I spent years researching the colors, changing them until I was happy with them," Bill says. He studied books, including *Victorian Exterior Decoration*, by Roger W. Moss and Gail Caskey Winkler, in which the authors explain "How to Paint Your Nineteenth-Century American House Historically." He went back to early paint palettes, researching color plates from old paint companies. Finally he settled on seven historically compatible colors for the house. Their Victorian names are Indian Red (the only original color, which he found under layers of white paint), Light Blue Green (the main color of the house), Dark Blue Green, Old Gold, Bronze Green, Shutter Green, and Buff.

The results are stunning. Everywhere one looks, a complex yet harmonious color scheme emerges, from the fretwork brackets beneath the windows to the elegant rafters in the porch roof. Each pattern is different—floral, geometric, diamond-shaped—the dentils and balustrades adding linear elements to the overall composition. The Gothic-style window opening onto the second-floor deck, with its pointed shutters, adds a final colorful flourish to the façade. There is no record of who did the dazzling carpentry work, but he deserves a posthumous honor for his extraordinary craftsmanship. Meanwhile, Bill and Marcina Wagner should rightly be honored, not only for their respect for this unknown artist, but for their meticulous restoration of what is undoubtedly one of the shore's most delightful cottages.

ABOVE LEFT *At every turn a masterpiece of carpentry has been rescued from oblivion and given the attention it deserves by Rosemere Cottage's proud owners.*
ABOVE RIGHT *The unknown craftsman who made these brackets and rafters should be given a chapter in the history books for his contribution to American vernacular architecture.*

"BIRDSONG ABOUNDS, THE OCEAN HUMS ITS LULLABIES, AND THE SEA DISAPPEARS INTO THE SUNSHINE."

On seeing this house, the reader would surely suppose it to be an illustration for a children's fairy tale. The truth is almost as bewitching. Its owner, Esta Cassway, found it in the five-and-dime. "I wasn't looking for a second home," she says, explaining her unexpected reaction to the faded photo of a decrepit-looking shack in the store. But she knew at once that this was to be her home. "That's my house," she declared. Thus began the turning point of her life.

Esta Cassway is a writer, painter, and lyricist, and also a wife and mother of three sons. The family was devoted to boats, and summers were usually spent on the water, tacking and jibing in the middle of Barnegat Bay. But after one too many dangerous escapes, they decided to spend more time on dry land. Driving down Sunset Boulevard in Cape May Point, Esta saw cows grazing happily on sand dunes. "I'm home," she thought, surprised, not being a seashore lazy-hazy afternoon type of person.

"We bathed that first day at Nun's Beach, with the Sisters of St. Joseph," she recalls. "The dunes fronted their big old retreat and while some of the sisters frolicked in the sea, the older women in their black serge sat rocking, lined up in rows, on the many verandahs. It seemed otherworldly; a good introduction to the vagaries of life at Cape May Point." Shortly after, Esta saw the faded photo in the window of the aforementioned five-and-dime. Let Esta tell the rest of the story in her own words.

"The next day I found my way to the street where I now live. A rose-covered sand dune was at one end and trees and flowers lined the unpaved street. This was considered the seedy part of town, its cottages barely more than tent-like camp houses. My home-to-be was no exception, but for a white picket fence. Having spent a significant part of my youth visiting a shore house with a white picket fence, I am sure that fate and familiarity were guiding me. Later that day, I inveigled my architect husband to come and look down into the house by way of a window in the roof. This is what he said: 'I don't want another house. But if you can find out who owns this shack, then, well, maybe.' Big laugh. Little did he suspect the new me. By Tuesday morning I had found the owner, living on the east side of New York. Her dear husband had just died, having fallen down the steps, but, she said, he certainly would have approved. After all, that was how they got the house, tracking down and bugging the former owner till she sold. 'Come up with the money and it's yours.'

FACING *A dazzling performance of roses, hydrangeas, lilies, platycodon, and other profusely flowering plants announces to the world that this is the entrance to Terning Point Cottage—or perhaps the beginning of a fairy tale.*

ABOVE *The rear of the house, with simple louvers, gated storage, and stairs going up to the second floor, shows how very small the lot actually is.* **FACING** *At the back of the house, hydrangeas and daylilies are some of the thirty or so different plants that cozy up to each other, reaching up to the second-floor bedroom.*

"The only condition of sale was the assurance, by the strict one-man zoning commission of Cape May Point, that an addition would be allowed. The house is on an undersized lot, twenty-five feet by one hundred feet, and newer building codes are in effect. The fourteen-by-sixteen-foot original house was built 120 years ago; its construction defies all logical engineering laws. The three-quarter-inch-thick walls are made of Philadelphia fencing, peepholes included. It is a permanent tent, canvas-covered at one time, the wood added later. Because of the lack of traditional construction, the gabled roof is held together by red quarter-inch cable wire. The windows open in, not out. The sophisticated heating system is a Franklin stove; portable heaters, subject to the whims of wiring, move with the tenants from room to room like pet dogs.

"The kitchen, as we found it, was two boards into which a sink had been nailed; the

former owners mostly partook of liquid refreshments. Two flat doors covered with mattresses made up the bedroom suite, also located in this charming kitchen area."

The weekend after settlement, Esta's architect husband and son Nick gutted the entire mess and installed a simple, workable kitchen based on the premise that meals would be simple and workable; a cook-top, a sink, and a small refrigerator would suffice. "Over the years, a large refrigerator, self-cleaning oven, microwave, dishwasher, ice-cream maker, electric fry pan, wok, juicer, and an outside gas grill have miraculously appeared. Miraculous because if they hadn't appeared, no one would have eaten.

"This was an efficiency house. There were no bedrooms. The living room and five-foot porch became sleeping space for five, with flip-out beds and loft—rather like those boats I'd like to forget. An addition was soon under construction. My husband designed a sleeping tower, with building forms reminiscent of the original house. This fit the allowable buildable space—two stories high and ten feet wide. My personal retreat and bedroom is up a narrow stair, enclosed by eye-level trees. Birdsong abounds, the ocean hums its lullabies, and the sea disappears into the sunshine.

"Interior decoration is a big thing in Cape May Point. Every June there is a large junk pick-up. The night before, certain residents are seen cruising the Point looking for throwaways. They load these found objects into cars and beach wagons, spend the summer trying to figure out where to put them, and then put them out in the October junk pick-up. This is called recycling. Most owners decorate their cottages with treasures from yard sales and antique flea markets. I have never heard of anyone in this town hiring a decorator. Terning Point Cottage has antique wicker rockers, chintz pillows, paintings, prints and photos (most of these by the owners), samplers, candlewicks, and lots of flower vases. Everyone else's

ABOVE LEFT *Esta Cassway uses containers of variegated, white, and red impatiens to add color and shape to the more shady corners of the garden.*
ABOVE RIGHT *A combination of Buff Beauty and New Dawn roses, hardy in this tough salt- and wind-laden climate, tumble down in exuberant garlands over the white picket fence.*
FACING *Inside the cottage, Esta Cassway's artistic talents infuse every wall, every sitting space, every fabric, every object.*

cottage has just about the same accouterments, from the same yard sales and antique markets. We like each other's taste."

While Esta and her family have transformed the interior of their shack into a wonderland of summer living, the garden has also been touched by Esta's magic wand. "For twenty-three years, my summer garden has been a hardy, disease-resistant testament to what will grow at the seashore. The addition of topsoil, peat moss, and plant food, mixed with the sandy soil, and the help of frogs, box turtles, butterflies, hummingbirds, and finches, have created a perfect environment, lush and fragrant. After ducking under a low arbor of climbing New Dawn and Buff Beauty roses, you enter a secret garden filled with oriental lilies, daylilies, huge shrub roses, Annabelle hydrangeas, and blue plumbago auriculata. At least thirty different varieties of plants vie for attention in this tiny home. The garden at Terning Point is a joy to live with, each blossom like the sun rising on a new day."

At the end of summer, when the warblers gather for the flight south, the purple martins have disappeared, and the box turtles have found a warm spot in the woods, Esta Cassway begins the slow process of putting the house to bed for the winter. "The hammock is rolled up and window screens have been washed and put away. Soon this little cottage will withstand another assault from winter, although in Cape May Point the ground rarely freezes. Perhaps it recalls the love it has known and keeps the warmth of that memory within.

" 'Goodbye, little house,' I say. 'Take care of yourself and remember me.' "

ABOVE LEFT *The adjacent cottage (since demolished) shows the extent of the transformation occurring next door.*

ABOVE RIGHT *The original Terning Point Cottage—like its neighbor, a tent-like shack, originally canvas-covered— has become a magical summer family hideaway.*

FACING *The cottage may be tiny, but the garden that surrounds it is a horticultural encyclopedia, each flower contributing its color and scent to the intoxicating whole.*

BIBLIOGRAPHY

Benedict, Anne L. *Mantoloking Through the Lens*. Mantoloking, N.J.: Mantoloking Historical Society, 2001.

Buchholz, Margaret Thomas, ed. *Shore Chronicles: Diaries and Travelers' Tales from the Jersey Shore, 1764–1955*. Harvey Cedars, N.J.: Down the Shore Publishing, 1999.

Colt, George Howe. *The Big House: A Century in the Life of an American Summer Home*. New York: Scribners, 2003.

Cunningham, John T. *The New Jersey Shore*. New Brunswick, N.J.: Rutgers University Press, 1958.

Genovese, Peter. *The Jersey Shore Uncovered: A Revealing Season on the Beach*. New Brunswick, N.J.: Rutgers University Press, 2003.

Guthorn, Peter J. *The Sea Bright Skiff and Other Jersey Shore Boats*. New Brunswick, N.J.: Rutgers University Press, 1971.

Hoffmann, Sue Johnson, and Jeanne M. Wenzel. *The History of Lavallette 1887–1997*. Lavallette, N.J.: Lavallette Heritage Committee, 1997.

Javellana, René, Fernando Nakpil Zialcita, and Elizabeth W. Reyes. *Filipino Style*. Singapore: Archipelago Press, [1997] 2005.

Karch, Mary. *Under the Lighthouse: Memories of Barnegat City*. Harvey Cedars, N.J.: Down the Shore Publishing, 2004.

Kobbé, Gustav. *The New Jersey Coast and Pines: An Illustrated Guide-book with Road Maps*. 1889; reprint, Baltimore: Gateway Press, 1970.

Kunstler, William Moses. *The Minister and the Choir Singer: The Hall-Mills Murder Case*. New York: Morrow, 1964.

Moss, Roger W., and Gail Caskey Winkler. *Victorian Exterior Decoration: How to Paint Your Nineteenth-Century American House Historically*. New York: Henry Holt and Co., 1987, 1992.

Nash, Charles Edgar. *The Lure of Long Beach*. [Long Beach, N.J.]: Long Beach Island Board of Trade, 1936.

Robert, Russell, and Richard Youmans. *Down the Jersey Shore*. New Brunswick, N.J.: Rutgers University Press, 1994.

Rose, T. E., H. C. Woolman, and T. T. Price. *Historical and Biographical Atlas of the New Jersey Coast*. Philadelphia: Woolman & Rose, 1878; reprint, Toms River, N.J.: Ocean County Historical Society, 1985.

Ruset, Ben. "Greetings from Asbury Park." Available at http://www.NJPineBarrens.com/content/view/22/40.

Ryan, Michael. *Secret Life: An Autobiography*. New York: Vintage, 1996.

Santelli, Robert. *Guide to the Jersey Shore: From Sandy Hook to Cape May*. Old Saybrook, Conn.: Globe Pequot Press, 1998.

Savadore, Larry, and Margaret Thomas Buchholz. *Great Storms of the Jersey Shore*. Harvey Cedars, N.J.: Down the Shore Publishing and The SandPiper, 1993.

Schoettle, William C. *Bay Head 1879–1911*. Bay Head, N.J.: Pickering Press, 1966.

Somerville, George B. *The Lure of Long Beach*. Harvey Cedars, N.J.: Down the Shore Publishing, 1995.

The Story of Asbury Park: The Record of Achievement, 1916–1931. 1931; Asbury Park, N.J.: Asbury Park Historical Society, 2002.

Wolff, Daniel. *4th of July, Asbury Park: A History of the Promised Land*. New York: Bloomsbury Press, 2005.

Wrege, Charles D. *Spring Lake: An Early History*. Spring Lake, N.J.: Bicentennial History Committee, 1976.

INDEX

Page numbers in *italic* indicate photographs.

ABOUT THE AUTHOR AND PHOTOGRAPHER

CAROLINE SEEBOHM is the author of several illustrated books on architecture and design, including *Great Houses and Gardens of New Jersey* (Rutgers University Press), *Boca Rococo: How Addison Mizner Invented Florida's Gold Coast* and *Under Live Oaks: The Last Great Houses of the Old South*. She has also published three biographies and two novels, the most recent being *The Innocents*.

PETER C. COOK is an award-winning photographer who specializes in architecture and portraiture.

Produced by Wilsted & Taylor Publishing Services
Project management by Christine Taylor
Production by Jennifer Uhlich and Andrew Patty
Copyediting by Nancy Evans
Composition by Yvonne Tsang
Printer's devilment by Lillian Marie Wilsted